Macbook Pi

Air

for Seniors

An Illustrated Simple Step By Step Guide For Beginners

Maddison Foster

Table of Contents

GETTING STARTED WITH YOUR MACBOOK   6

TURNING ON YOUR MACBOOK!   8

CHARGING YOUR MACBOOK   10

SETTING UP YOUR MAC   12

MANAGING YOUR APPLE ID   14

PERSONALIZE YOUR DESKTOP BACKGROUND AND APPEARANCE   16

DESKTOP, MENU BAR, AND HELP FEATURES ON MAC   18

FINDER   20

THE DOCK   22

NOTIFICATION CENTRE   24

CONTROL CENTRE   25

SYSTEM SETTINGS   27

SPOTLIGHT ON YOUR MAC   28

MANAGING YOUR WINDOWS ON YOUR MAC!   31

MIGRATING YOUR DATA   34

TRANSFER DATA TO A NEW MACBOOK MIGRATION ASSISTANT   36

HOW TO BACKUP YOUR MACBOOK USING TIME MACHINE   38

RESORING YOUR MACBOOK TO ITS ORIGINAL SETTING   38

MAC AND OTHER APPLE CONNECTIVITY   42

AIRDROP ON YOUR MAC   42

APPLE PAY ON YOUR MAC AND OTHER DEVICES   46

HOTSPOT CONTINUITY   46

CONTINUITY CAMERA   47

APPLE ID AND ICLOUD   50

HANDOFF TO ON YOUR MAC   53

USING UNIVERSAL CLIPBOARD ACROSS APPLE DEVICES   55

PHONE CALL AND TEXT FROM YOUR MAC   57

UNLOCKING YOUR MAC USING YOUR APPLE WATCH   60

AIRPRINT   61

APPS   62

BOOKS   66

CALENDAR   68

FACETIME   70

FIND MY APP   72

FREE FORM   74

HOME   76

MAIL   78

MAPS   81

MESSAGES   86

MUSIC   90

NEWS   93

NOTES   97

PHOTOS   102

PODCASTS   108

PREVIEW   110

REMINDERS   111

SAFARI   113

APPLE TV   120

VOICE MEMOS   124

GETTING STARTED WITH YOUR MACBOOK

Open up your Macbook and to get started!
Set up your new Mac in a few simple steps.

HARDWARE OVERVIEW

MACBOOK AIR

FaceTime HD camera

Do Not Disturb

Dictation

Spotlight

MagSafe 3

Thunderbolt / USB 4

Touch ID

Force Touch trackpad

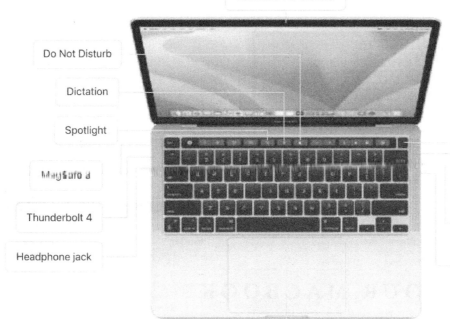

FaceTime HD camera

Do Not Disturb

Dictation

Spotlight

MagSafe 3

Thunderbolt 4

Headphone jack

Touch ID

HDMI port

Thunderbolt 4 (USB-C)

SDXC card slot

Force Touch trackpad

SOFTWARE OVERVIEW

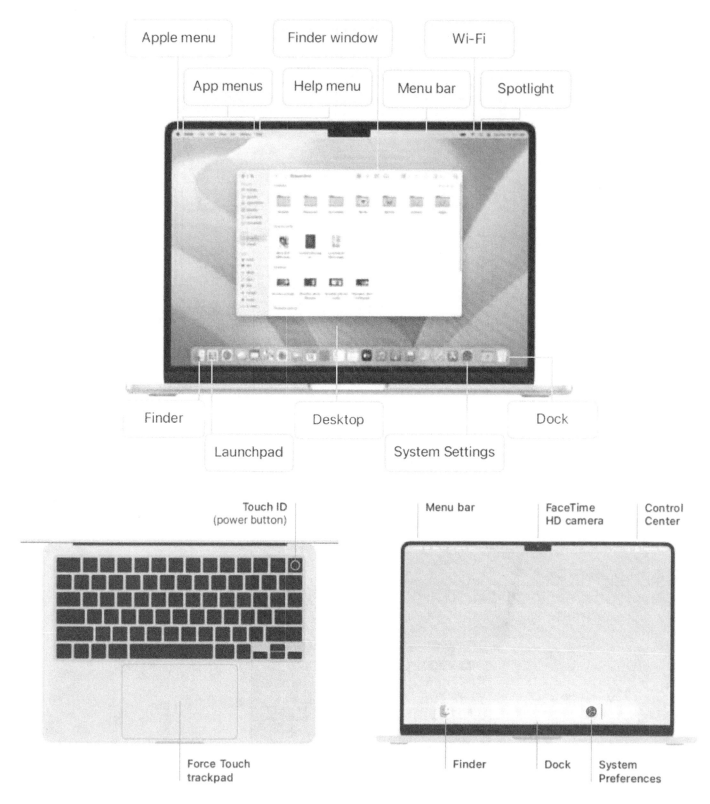

TURNING ON YOUR MACBOOK!

A Simple Guide to Starting Up Your MacBook
Step 1: Locate the Power Button
The power button can be found at the top-right corner of your keyboard.

Step 2: Turn on Your MacBook
Press the power button gently. You may hear a chime (on older MacBook models) or see your screen light up.

Step 3: Wait for Start-Up
Your MacBook will begin the start-up process. The Apple logo will appear on your screen. The time it takes for your MacBook to start up depends on its specific model.

Step 4: Sign In
Once start-up is complete, a prompt will appear asking for your username and password (if you have set these up). Follow the instructions on your screen to sign in.

Step 5: You're Ready to Go
After successfully signing in, you will be taken to your desktop. Your MacBook is now fully operational and ready for use.

Note: It's important to shut down your MacBook properly when you're finished using it. To do this, click on the Apple icon in the top-left corner of your screen and select "Shut Down." This ensures that all active programs and processes are safely closed.

Charge with MagSafe 3

1. Plug the USB-C power adaptor into a plug socket.

2. Plug the USB-C end of the MagSafe 3 cable into the power adaptor.

3. Connect the other end of the cable to the MagSafe 3 port on your Mac.

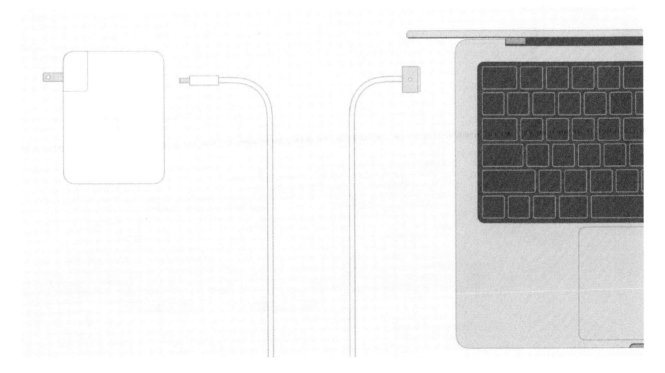

CHARGING YOUR MACBOOK

For MagSafe 3 Port Users:

1. Identify the MagSafe 3 Port: This port is located on the left side of your MacBook, near the escape key.
2. How to Charge Using MagSafe 3:
- Insert the Power Adapter: Plug the USB-C power adapter into an electrical outlet.
- Connect the Cable: Link the USB-C side of the MagSafe 3 cable to the power adapter you just plugged in.
- Attach to MacBook: Connect the opposite end of the cable to your MacBook's MagSafe 3 port.
3. Check Charging Status: After linking the charger, observe the indicator light. A green glow indicates a full battery, while an amber light indicates the battery is either charging or paused in the charging process.

Note: MagSafe 3 charging is compatible with the following MacBook models:

- MacBook Air released in 2022 and onwards
- 14-inch MacBook Pro launched in 2021 and later
- 16-inch MacBook Pro introduced in 2021 and subsequent models

9. Set Up Touch ID:

- If your MacBook Pro supports Touch ID, you can add your fingerprint during setup. To configure Touch ID later or add more fingerprints, go to System Settings > Touch ID & Password. To add a fingerprint, click the ➕ button and follow the onscreen instructions. You can use Touch ID for various purposes, such as unlocking your Mac and making purchases.

10. Apple Pay setup (optional): One user account can set up Apple Pay. Additional users can link their iPhone or Apple Watch for payments.

11. Desktop mode: Choose between Light, Dark, or Auto for your desktop. Changes can be made later in System Preferences.

You can opt to skip some steps and return to them later, ensuring a personalized setup experience.

APPLE ID ON MAC

Your Apple ID is a crucial account that grants access to a range of Apple services. You can utilize it to download apps from the App Store, access media in Apple Music, Apple Podcasts, Apple TV, and Apple Books, synchronize content across devices using iCloud, create a Family Sharing group, and much more.

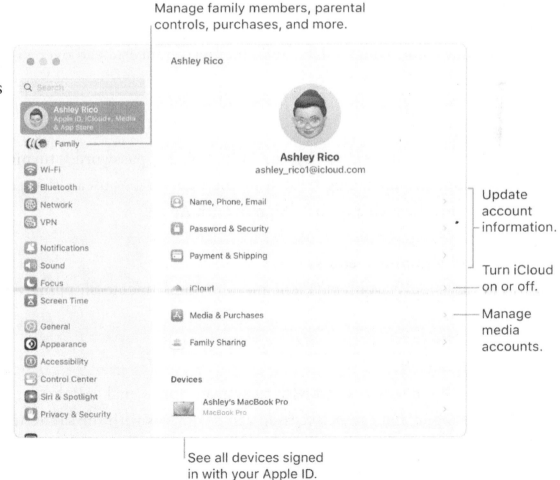

Manage family members, parental controls, purchases, and more.

Update account information.

Turn iCloud on or off.

Manage media accounts.

See all devices signed in with your Apple ID.

MANAGING YOUR APPLE ID

Retrieving a Lost Password

If you happen to forget your Apple ID password, don't create a new account. Instead, click "Forgot Apple ID or password?" during sign-in process to recover it.

Family Account Setup

Each family member who uses Apple products should have their own Apple ID. You can set up IDs for your children and use Family Sharing to distribute purchases and subscriptions.

Accessing Apple ID Settings

You can control all aspects of your Apple ID via System Preferences on your MacBook. Find your Apple ID and Family Sharing options at the top of the sidebar. To sign in, click "Sign in with your Apple ID."

Modifying Your Account Details

To revise your name, contact data, and email preferences, head over to System Preferences and click on your Apple ID.

Security Options

Keep your account secure by updating your password, turning on two-factor authentication, and managing trusted phone numbers. You can also generate verification codes and control which apps use "Sign in with Apple."

Payment and Shipping Details

You can also modify your payment methods and update shipping addresses for Apple Store transactions.

iCloud Preferences

Choose the iCloud services you wish to activate. Once enabled, the corresponding content is stored in iCloud and can be accessed across devices with the same Apple ID.

Media and Purchasing Preferences

Oversee accounts associated with Apple Music, Podcasts, TV, and Books. Tweak purchasing configurations and manage your subscriptions.

Device Management

Check all devices connected to your Apple ID. Ensure that "Find My [device]" is active for each and review iCloud Backup status for iOS or iPadOS gadgets. Remove devices you no longer possess.

Family Sharing Configuration

Create a family group of up to six members to share purchases, locate devices, and employ "Find My" functionalities. Monitor your children's device usage and set Screen Time restrictions.

Account Recovery and Posthumous Access

Designate recovery contacts or generate a recovery key for easier password resets. Appoint trusted people as Legacy Contacts to access your account and private information after your lifetime.

Your Apple ID serves as an all-in-one gateway for various Apple services, allowing you to streamline and manage your digital activities effectively.

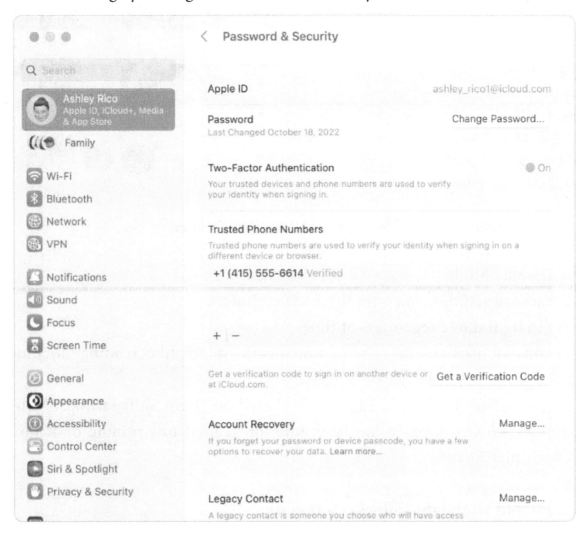

PERSONALIZE YOUR DESKTOP BACKGROUND AND APPEARANCE

You have the option to select a basic color, use a favorite image, or even set a scenic photo that transitions with the time of day.

Setting Your Desktop Wallpaper

1. Click the Apple menu icon located at the top-left corner of your display.
2. Select "System Preferences."
3. Within System Preferences, find "Wallpaper" on the sidebar. Scroll if needed and click it.

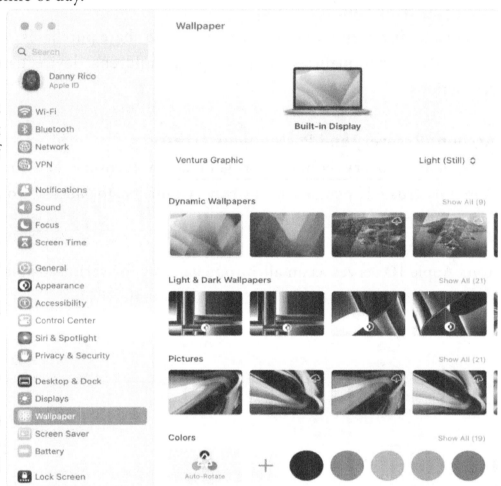

Adjusting Display Appearance

1. 1. Go to the Apple menu at the top-left of your screen and select "System Preferences."
2. 2. Click "Appearance" icon within System Preferences.

Choosing Display Mode

In the Appearance settings, you have three main choices:

Light: Stays in light mode regardless of time.

Dark: Remains in dark mode. Useful for specific tasks like reading documents and browsing the web.

Auto: Switches between light and dark modes based on Night Shift settings. Note that the switch happens when your Mac has been idle for at least one minute or if no apps are keeping the display awake.

Select Accent and Highlight Colors (Optional)

Within Appearance settings, you can choose an accent color for buttons and menus. You can also pick a highlight color for selected text.

Dynamic Wallpapers

Certain dynamic wallpapers offer still images to match your light or dark setting. For example, if you select dark mode during setup, a dark still image becomes your wallpaper. To change this, go back to "Change Wallpaper settings."

Quick Dark Mode Access

For a fast switch to Dark Mode, use Control Center. Click its icon in the menu bar, proceed to "Display," and finally select "Dark Mode."

Your desktop appearance represents your preferences. Customize it to give your MacBook a unique look.

Choose the color scheme for your Mac.

Click an item in the sidebar to adjust settings.

DESKTOP, MENU BAR, AND HELP FEATURES ON MAC

The desktop is the first thing you see on your MacBook. It's where you can access apps, search for items on your Mac and the web, organize your files, and more.

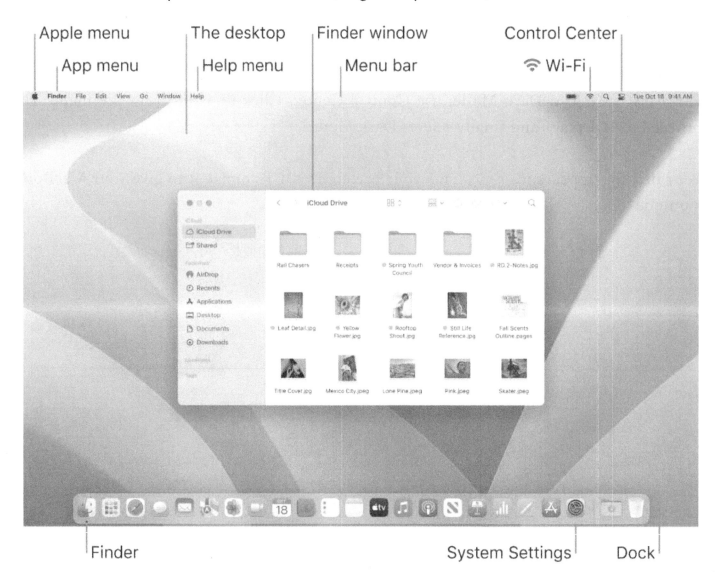

Menu Bar

- The menu bar is located at the top of your screen and provides various commands and functions for apps. The available options change depending on the app you're using. The right side of the menu bar features task-related icons such as Wi-Fi connectivity 🛜 battery status 🔋Control Center access ⚙ and Spotlight search🔍

Apple Menu

In the upper-left corner, you'll find the Apple menu. This menu holds items you frequently use. A simple click on the Apple icon 🍎 opens this menu.

App Menu

The name of the app you're currently using appears in bold, next to the Apple menu . Directly below, you'll see menus specific to that app. The app's unique menus are listed below. When you switch apps or windows, the app menu and other menus on the menu bar will change accordingly.

Help Menu

The Help menu is always available via the menu bar. To access it, open the Finder from the Dock, navigate to the Help menu, and choose "macOS Help" to open the macOS User Guide. Additionally, you can search for topics by typing in the provided search field. For guidance specific to an app, open that app and select "Help" from the menu bar.

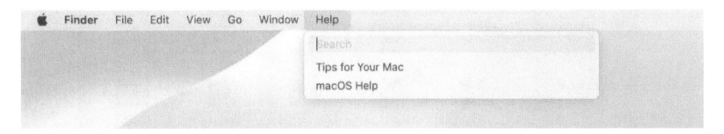

Organizing with Stacks

Using the Stacks feature is an excellent way to keep your desktop organized. Stacks group files, and you can sort them by type, date, or tags. Click on a stack to reveal its files; hover to view file thumbnails. To initiate Stacks, click on the desktop, then go to "View > Use Stacks." You can further categorize stacks by selecting "View > Group Stacks By." Files newly added to the desktop will automatically sort into the correct stack.

By understanding these elements, you can efficiently navigate your MacBook's desktop and manage your files.

FINDER

How to Open a Finder Window

To open a Finder window on your Mac, click on the blue, smiley face Finder icon located in the Dock at the bottom of your screen.

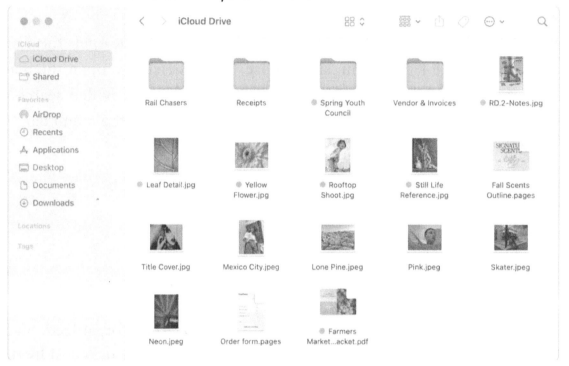

Navigating Within the Finder

Once you have opened the Finder window, you can view your folders and files in different ways, such as icons, list, hierarchical columns, or gallery. To switch between these views, click the pop-up menu button located at the top of the Finder window.

The Sidebar Overview

The left-hand sidebar within the Finder window provides easy access to frequently accessed items, such as your iCloud Drive folder, which displays your iCloud-stored documents. To adjust what appears here, go to Finder > Preferences.

Organizing Your Folders

Your Mac comes with predefined folders, such as Documents, Pictures, Applications, and Music, which are designated for specific content. To create additional folders for better organization, go to File > New Folder.

Device Synchronization

When you connect external devices like an iPhone or iPad to your Mac, they will appear in the Finder's sidebar. Click on the device's name to explore options for backup, updating, and restoring.

Utilizing Gallery View

Gallery View provides a large preview of your selected files, which is useful for identifying pictures, video clips, and other visual documents. The Preview pane to the right offers additional file details, and a scrubber bar at the bottom aids in quick file navigation.

Quick Actions in Gallery View

In Gallery View, you can use the "More" button ⋯ found at the bottom right to access quick action shortcuts. You can perform various tasks like rotating photos, cropping or annotating images using Markup, combining files, trimming audio and video clips, and even running custom actions created with the Shortcuts app or Automator workflows.

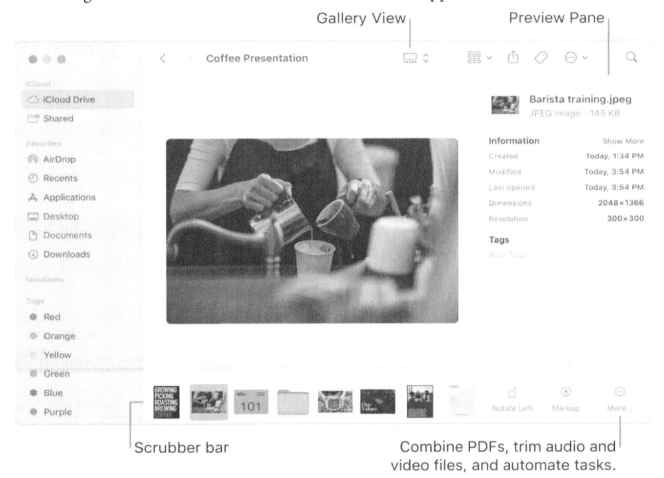

Gallery View · Preview Pane

Scrubber bar

Combine PDFs, trim audio and video files, and automate tasks.

Using Quick Look

To preview a file without opening it in a separate application, simply select the file and press the Space bar. This Quick Look feature lets you perform tasks like signing PDFs, trimming audio and video, or editing images.

Navigating via the Go Menu

The Go menu in the menu bar provides a convenient route for accessing folders and locations. For example, you can easily locate the Utilities folder by selecting Go > Utilities. Use Go > Enclosing Folder to climb to a parent folder, or Go > Go to Folder to enter a specific folder path.

The Finder's Features

The Finder is your central platform for organizing and accessing all your files, folders, and devices on your Mac. Its multiple features are designed to help you maintain organization and efficiency in your day-to-day operations.

THE DOCK

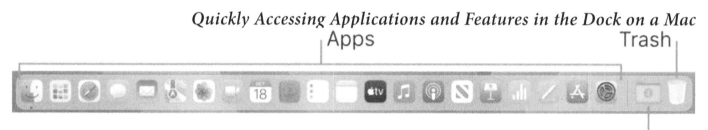

Quickly Accessing Applications and Features in the Dock on a Mac

The Dock on a Mac is a quick and easy way to access your favorite applications and features. Here are some tips on how to make the most of it:

Launching Applications

To launch an application, simply click on its icon in the Dock. For example, to open Finder, select its icon in the Dock.

Opening Files

To open a file using an application, drag the file onto the application's Dock icon. For instance, if you want to open a document using Pages, drag the document onto the Pages icon in the Dock.

Locating Items within Finder

To locate an item within Finder, use the Command-click function on its Dock icon.

Switching Between Apps

To switch back to the last-used app while hiding the active one, use Option-click on the current app's Dock icon. To switch to another app while concealing all other apps, use Option-Command-click on the intended app's icon.

Additional Dock Item Actions

To view more action options for a Dock item, Control-click the item's icon. A shortcut menu will appear, offering actions like "Show Recents" or allowing you to open files. If an application becomes unresponsive, force it to close by Control-clicking its Dock icon and selecting "Force Quit." Just be cautious, as unsaved changes may be lost.

Managing Items in the Dock

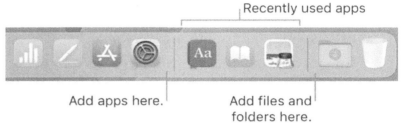

Recently used apps

Add apps here.

Add files and folders here.

To add an item to the Dock, drag apps to the left-hand side of the separator line and files or folders to the right-hand side. This will place an alias for the item in the Dock. To remove an item, simply drag it off the Dock until a "Remove" prompt appears. Note that this only removes the alias, not the actual item. If an app icon is accidentally removed from the Dock, it can be restored. Open the app to have its icon reappear in the Dock, then Control-click the icon and select "Options" > "Keep in Dock." Rearranging items within the Dock is straightforward; just drag an item to its desired new position.

Customizing the Dock

To modify how the Dock looks and operates, go to the Apple menu > System Preferences, and then click on "Desktop & Dock" found in the sidebar (scrolling might be necessary to locate it). Within "Dock" preferences, you can adjust the Dock's appearance, size, and location (either at the bottom, left, or right edge of your screen). The Dock can also be hidden if desired. If you need additional guidance on customization options, click the "Help" button ? located at the bottom of the window.

Keyboard Shortcuts for Dock Navigation

You can quickly alter the Dock's size by hovering over the separator line until a double arrow appears; then click and drag upwards or downwards. To use keyboard shortcuts for Dock navigation, press Control-F3 (or Control-Fn-F3 on a laptop) to shift focus to the Dock. Utilize the Left and Right Arrow keys to move between icons and press Return to open a selected item.

Notifications in the Dock

A red badge appearing on an app's Dock icon signals pending actions or notifications, such as unread emails in the Mail app .

NOTIFICATION CENTRE

Your Mac's Control Panel for Notifications and Widgets

1. Accessing the Notification Center

- Click on the date and time or swipe left using two fingers from the right edge of the trackpad to access the Notification Center.
- To exit the Notification Center, click on the desktop, click on the date and time again, or swipe right with two fingers on your trackpad.

3. Managing Notifications

- View or minimize multiple notifications from one app by clicking on the topmost notification to expand them or clicking "Show less" ⌄ to minimize the stack.

Click the date and time to open Notification Centre.

See notifications you missed and keep track of your day.

Customise widgets.

- Respond to a notification directly by clicking its action button, such as "Snooze" for a Calendar notification or "Reply" for an email notification.
- Click on the small arrow next to a notification to reveal additional options, such as replying with a message if you decide to decline an incoming call.
- Access more information related to a notification by clicking on the notification itself. If a small arrow ⟩ appears next to the app name, clicking it will unveil further details.
- Change the settings for notifications from a specific app by clicking the ⟩ button next to the app name, followed by the preferences button ● ● ● Here you can choose options such as muting or turning off notifications, or go into the app's notification settings.
- Remove a notification or clear a stack by clicking the "Clear" button ⊗.

3. Interacting with Widgets

- Click anywhere within a widget to open related settings or apps. For example, clicking the Clock widget takes you to the Date & Time settings, while clicking the Weather widget opens your web browser to a full weather forecast.
- Control-click the widget in the Notification Center and select a different size to adjust the size of a widget.
- Hover over a widget while holding down the Option key and then click the "Remove" button ⊖ to remove a widget.

The Notification Center serves as your command center for both notifications and widgets, offering you an organized way to interact with timely and important information.

CONTROL CENTRE

Mastering the Control Center: Quick Access to Your Mac's Settings and Tools

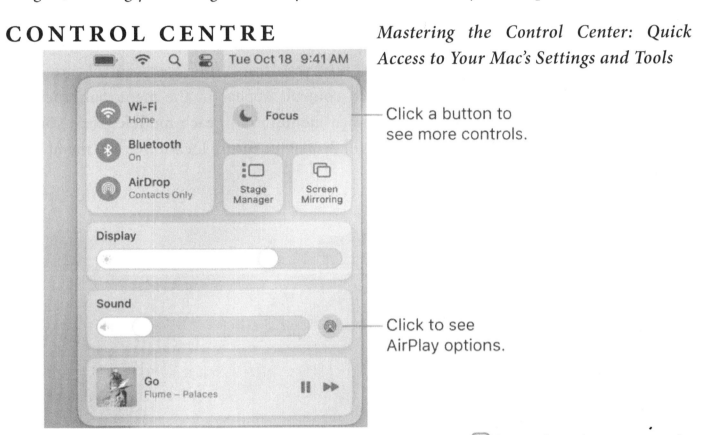

To access the Control Center on your Mac, click on its icon located in the upper-right corner of your screen. The icon looks like a group of symbols.

Exploring Additional Options

Once you open the Control Center, clicking on any button will display a range of related options. For instance, clicking on the Wi-Fi symbol will show you available networks, saved networks, or even let you delve into Wi-Fi settings. You can go back to the main Control Center panel by clicking its icon once more.

Organize with Stage Manager

Stage Manager is a useful feature that lets you arrange your open apps and windows in a unified view. You can also group apps to form workspaces tailored to your needs, facilitating a more efficient management of multiple apps and windows.

Monitoring Your Microphone

The Control Center includes a recording indicator, letting you know when your Mac's microphone is currently in use or has been used recently. This feature bolsters your privacy and security by making you aware of apps that are accessing your microphone.

Quick Access to Favorite Controls

To pin your most-used controls directly to the menu bar, simply drag your desired Control Center item to the menu bar. This way, your frequently used controls are just a click away. If you want to customize which controls appear in the menu bar, open the Control Center settings and use the dropdown menu next to each module. Here you can select "Show in Menu Bar", and a preview will display its future location in the menu bar.

Deleting Items from the Menu Bar

If you wish to remove an item from the menu bar, hold down the Command key and drag the item away from the menu bar.

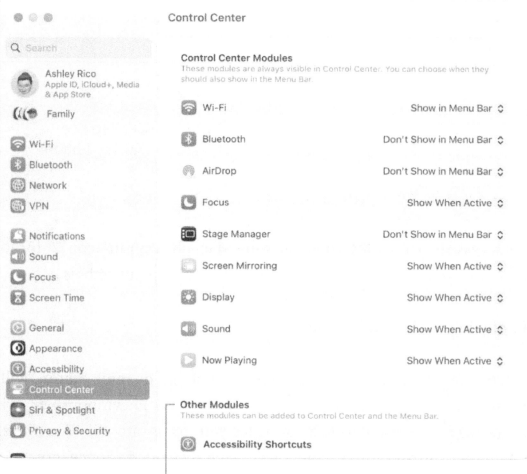

Choose additional modules to add to Control Center.

SYSTEM SETTINGS

Navigating System Preferences; Your Guide to Personalizing Your Mac

Accessing System Preferences

To get to System Preferences, you have a couple of options:

- Click on the System Preferences icon located in the Dock.
- Go to the Apple menu in the top-left corner of your screen and select "System Preferences." From there, you can pick the specific setting you wish to modify from the sidebar.

Personalizing Your Mac

System Preferences provides an array of settings to help you customize your Mac experience. These include, but are not limited to:

- Sleep Settings: Set the timing for when your Mac should enter sleep mode.
- Desktop Background: Choose a personalized background image for your desktop.
- Display Modes: Select between light, dark, or automatic mode for your Mac's interface.

To make any changes, click on the particular setting listed in the sidebar that you want to personalize. Some settings may be lower down, so you may need to scroll to see them.

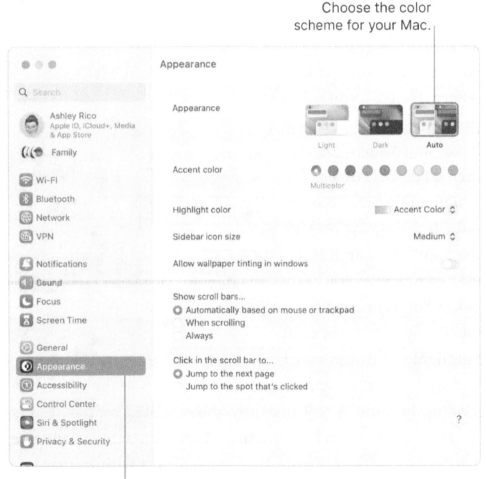

Choose the color scheme for your Mac.

Click an item in the sidebar to adjust settings.

Keeping macOS Up to Date

You can also manage your macOS updates through System Preferences. Follow these steps:

- In the System Preferences window, click on "General."
- Next, click on "Software Update" to see if your Mac has the latest macOS version.
- Here, you can also set your preferences for automatic updates.
- System Preferences is your go-to destination for tailoring your MacBook to your needs and ensuring it's running the most current macOS software. This feature is essential for efficiently managing your Mac's configuration and appearance.

SPOTLIGHT ON YOUR MAC

Spotlight is a quick-search feature on your Mac that can help you find almost anything on your computer. Here's everything you need to know about using Spotlight.

Accessing Spotlight

To access Spotlight, simply click on the magnifying glass icon located at the top right corner of your screen. Alternatively, you can press the F4 key if you have a 14-inch or 16-inch MacBook or use the Command-Space bar to quickly bring up or hide the Spotlight search field.

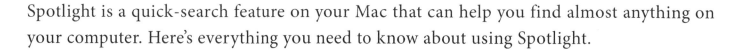

Start typing, and results appear quickly.

What You Can Search

Once you've opened Spotlight, you can start typing what you're looking for, and it will instantly show related search results. You can search for a wide range of content such as pictures, files, contacts, calendar events, and emails. Spotlight also has a Live Text feature that can find text within images, although it may not work for all languages.

Launching Applications

If you want to open an application quickly, just type its name into Spotlight and press the Return key when it appears in the search results.

Performing Quick Actions

You can also use Spotlight to carry out tasks like activating a shortcut, enabling a Focus mode, or initiating a timer without launching other applications. To perform these quick actions, simply type the desired action into Spotlight.

Currency and Unit Conversion

Spotlight can also be used to convert currencies and measurements. Enter a currency symbol and amount, and it will display the converted values. For unit conversions, simply specify a unit, and the converted result will appear.

Siri Suggestions

Spotlight includes Siri Suggestions, which offer information from various online sources like articles, search results, news, and more.

Personalizing Spotlight

If you want to personalize Spotlight's search preferences, you can do so through "System Preferences > Siri & Spotlight." You can uncheck the box next to "Siri Suggestions" if you only want Spotlight to search local files.

Siri is a voice-activated assistant available on your MacBook. Here are the steps to enable and use Siri on your MacBook:

1. Open your MacBook's "System Preferences."
2. Select "Siri & Spotlight."
3. Configure your Siri settings by choosing your preferred language and voice.

To activate Siri, you can follow the below steps based on your MacBook model:

1. On a 13-inch MacBook Pro: Tap the Siri icon in the Touch Bar's Control Strip or use Command-Space bar.
2. On a 14-inch or 16-inch MacBook Pro: Press and hold the Dictation/Siri key (F5) or the microphone key to open Siri.

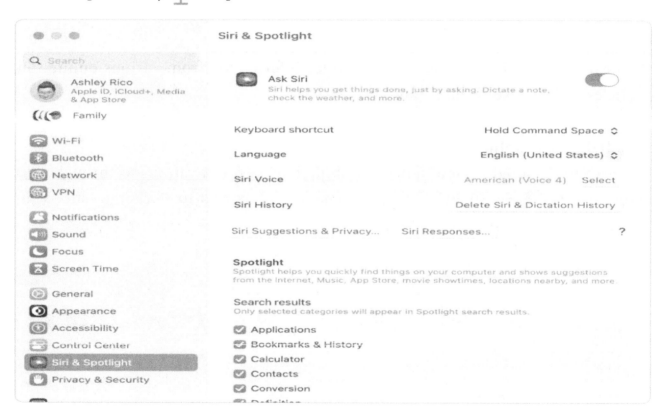

To set up voice activation, go to Siri settings and select "Listen for 'Hey Siri.'" Follow the setup guide. Once set up, say "Hey Siri" and your query. Note that this function is disabled when your MacBook's lid is closed.

Siri can assist you in various tasks, including but not limited to:
- Planning events and appointments
- Modifying settings
- Answering questions

- Text messaging and calling
- Adding calendar events
- Providing navigational directions
- Offering various informational tidbits
- Executing basic tasks, like list creation
- Playing music

Siri provides additional features such as drag and drop, which enables you to move images and locations from the Siri window into texts, emails, or documents. You can also customize Siri's voice by navigating to "Siri & Spotlight" in System Preferences and selecting a different option from the "Siri Voice" menu.

To know more about Siri's functionalities, simply ask Siri, "What can you do?" and you will be provided with a list of possible commands and actions.

MANAGING YOUR WINDOWS ON YOUR MAC!

Managing Windows on Your Mac: An Organized Approach

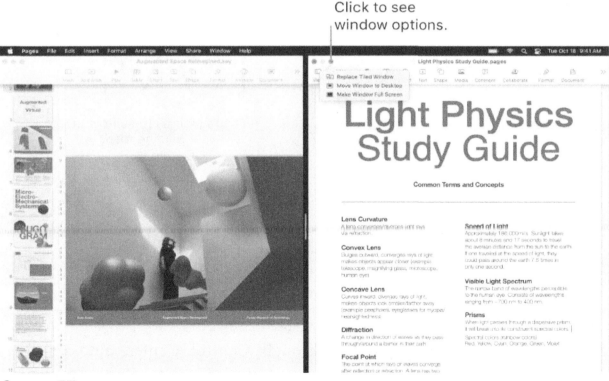

Full-Screen View

To let an application use the full screen, initiate full-screen mode.
- Hover the cursor over the green button at the upper-left of the application window.

- Select "Enter Full Screen" from the pop-up menu.

In this mode, the menu bar becomes invisible until you move the cursor to the screen's top. This feature is handy for applications like Keynote, Numbers, and Pages.

Split View

Split View lets you work with two applications simultaneously, each occupying half the screen.

- Hover over the green button in the upper-left corner of a window you wish to use in Split View.
- Select either "Tile Window to Left of Screen" or "Tile Window to Right of Screen" from the menu.
- Pick another window to fill the other half of the screen automatically.

Hovering over the green button will also provide additional options for switching between apps.

Stage Manager

The Stage Manager feature, accessible through Control Center, auto-arranges your applications and windows to minimize desktop clutter. The main window you're focusing on is positioned front and center, while others align on the sides for effortless access.

Mission Control

Mission Control offers a comprehensive view of all open windows, displayed on a single layer.

- Press the Mission Control key ▭▭ on your keyboard or use the Control-Up Arrow keys to access it.
- You can also place the Mission Control icon ◼◻ in the Dock for quicker reach.

This tool is particularly useful for swiftly locating and switching between open windows and desktop spaces.

Multiple Desktop Spaces

You can sort your application windows into various desktop spaces to segregate different tasks.

- Open Mission Control and click the "Add Desktop" button ╼╾ to create a new space.
- Navigate between these spaces using keyboard shortcuts or Mission Control.
- You also have the option to drag windows from one space to another.

Traffic Light Buttons

In every window's top-left corner, you'll find three buttons—red, yellow, and green—that serve distinct functions.

- Red: Closes the window. Some applications will also quit entirely.
- Yellow: Minimizes the window, which then moves to the right side of the Dock. Click it in the Dock to restore it.
- Green: Either expands the window to full-screen mode or initiates Split View, among other actions.

By understanding these features, you can effectively manage your windows and streamline your workflow on the Mac.

MIGRATING YOUR DATA

Migrating your data to a new MacBook can be a daunting task, but it doesn't have to be. This step-by-step guide will help you transfer your data to your new MacBook with ease.

Checking macOS Versions
First, ensure that your old computer has macOS 10.7 or a later version. If not, consider updating to the latest macOS for better compatibility.

Setting Up Your New MacBook
Confirm that your new MacBook has the latest macOS version installed. To verify, go to System Preferences > General > Software Update.

Wireless Data Transfer with Migration Assistant
- Open **Finder and go to Applications > Utilities.**
- **Double-click on the Migration Assistant application.**
- **Follow the prompts on the screen.**

- **Ensure** both computers are connected to the same Wi-Fi network and are in close proximity during the migration.

Data Transfer from Time Machine Backup

- If you've backed up your data using Time Machine on an external storage device, connect that device to your new MacBook.
- Drag and drop files directly from the external device onto your new MacBook.

Transferring Data from Another Mac

- Make sure both Macs are updated to the latest macOS version.
- Connect the two Macs using an Ethernet, FireWire, or Thunderbolt cable, or make sure they are on the same Wi-Fi network.
- On your new MacBook, open System Preferences, go to General, choose "Transfer or Reset," then click on "Open Migration Assistant."
- Click Continue and follow the onscreen instructions.
- On the older Mac, open Migration Assistant and follow the onscreen instructions.
- Choose what data you'd like to migrate:
  ▷ Applications
  ▷ User accounts with their specific content
  ▷ App data and files
  ▷ Computer settings
- Follow the remaining instructions and click Continue to start transferring data.

Transferring Data from a PC

- Make sure both the PC and the new MacBook are connected to the same network, either wired or wireless.
- Download and install the macOS version-compatible Windows Migration Assistant on your PC.
  - Close any running applications on your PC.
  - Launch the Windows Migration Assistant and follow the onscreen steps.
  - Select what data you'd like to migrate:
    ▷ User accounts and related content
    ▷ Computer settings
    ▷ Additional shared files and documents
- Click Continue to start the migration process.

Transferring Data from Time Machine Backup or Storage Device

- Connect your Time Machine backup or other storage device to your new MacBook.
- Open System Preferences, go to General, choose "Transfer or Reset," then click "Open Migration Assistant."
- Follow the onscreen instructions to select the data you wish to transfer.

After completing these steps, review the summary to ensure that all your data has been transferred without any issues. Click Done to close the Migration Assistant.

By following this guide, you'll be able to transfer your data to your new MacBook with ease and peace of mind.

TRANSFER DATA TO A NEW MACBOOK MIGRATION ASSISTANT

Migration Assistant   ×

Migration Assistant

Migration Assistant makes it easy to transfer your user accounts, which can include files, email messages, contacts and calendars, from your PC to a Mac. To begin, click Continue.

Quit   Continue

On Your New MacBook

1. Open Migration Assistant by going to Applications > Utilities.
2. Enter your administrator password when prompted.
3. Choose where to transfer data from: a Mac, Time Machine backup, or startup disk.

On Your Previous MacBook

1. Open Migration Assistant, which is located in the Utilities folder within the Applications folder.
2. Select the option to transfer data to another Mac and click "Continue."

Back on Your New MacBook

1. Select your old MacBook as the source for the transfer.
2. Wait for Migration Assistant to index the content on your old MacBook, which may take some time.
3. Choose the specific items you wish to transfer, such as user accounts, files, and folders.
4. Decide how to handle accounts with identical names on both MacBooks:
   - Rename: The account from the old MacBook will be added as a new user on the new MacBook.
   - Replace: The account on the new MacBook will be overwritten with the account from the old MacBook.
5. Click "Continue" to initiate the data transfer. Note that large transfers may take a considerable amount of time.

After the Transfer

1. Close Migration Assistant on both MacBooks.
2. Log in to the transferred account on your new MacBook to find your files and settings.

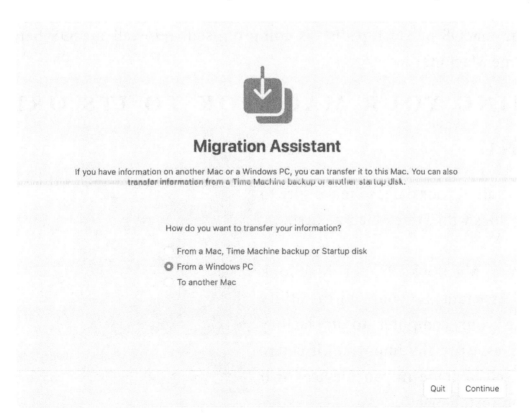

HOW TO BACKUP YOUR MACBOOK USING TIME MACHINE

Setting Up Time Machine

1. Make sure your MacBook and external storage device are on the same Wi-Fi network, or connect them directly.
2. Go to System Preferences > Time Machine and click "Select Backup Disk."
3. Choose the drive you want to use for the backup.

Additional Backup for iCloud

- For iCloud Drive: Go to System Preferences > Apple ID > iCloud and uncheck the "Optimize Mac Storage" box.
- For iCloud Photos: Open Photos, go to Photos > Preferences > iCloud and select "Download Originals to this Mac."

Restoring Files Using Time Machine

1. Click the Time Machine icon in the menu bar.
2. Select "Browse Other Time Machine Disks."
3. Choose the specific files, folders, or the entire disk that you want to restore. and tap restore.

Note: If your macOS or startup disk is compromised, reinstall macOS before restoring files with Time Machine.

RESORING YOUR MACBOOK TO ITS ORIGINAL SETTING

This will erase all of your data, so make sure to back up your files with Time Machine first.

If you own a MacBook Pro or MacBook Air, Erase Assistant is your go-to utility for restoring your computer to its factory settings. This is especially important if you're planning to sell or trade-in your device, or if you need to reinstall macOS.

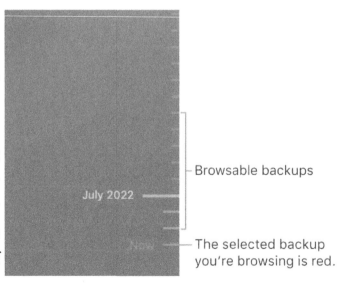

July 2022

Browsable backups

The selected backup you're browsing is red.

What Functions Does Erase Assistant Perform?

Erase Assistant carries out the following tasks:
- Signs you out of all Apple services, including iCloud.
- Disengages the "Find My" service and Activation Lock, removing the device from your Apple ID.
- Eliminates your personal settings, apps, and files.
- Clears all storage partitions, including any Windows installations created using Boot Camp Assistant.
- Eradicates all user accounts and the data associated with them.
- Here's How to Use Erase Assistant for Resetting Your MacBook:

1. Go to the Apple menu and choose System Preferences.
2. In the menu bar, pick System Preferences > Erase All Content and Settings.
3. In the Erase Assistant window, enter your administrator details.
4. Examine the list of elements that will be deleted, along with your own settings and files.
5. If you have more than one user account on your Mac, use the arrow next to your account name to view the items tied to those accounts.
6. Press "Continue" and adhere to the instructions that appear on your screen.

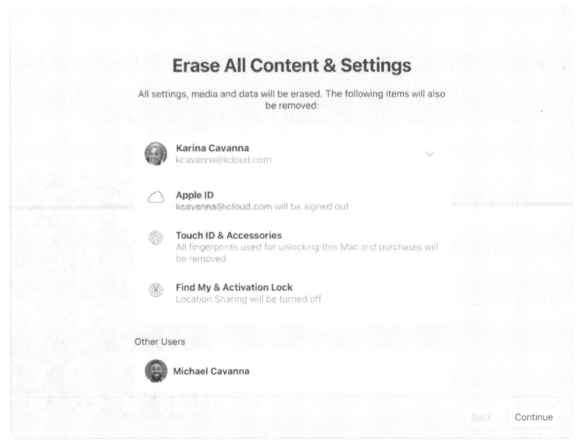

Dear Apple Pro!
I hope you are enjoying exploring the world of Apple devices thus far! Your feedback means a lot to me and it can be a valuable gift to fellow readers who are considering this guide. Writing a review on Amazon is a simple yet incredibly helpful

way to pay it forward. Scan this QR code to take you straight there!

Your words have the power to inspire confidence in others, just as I've aimed to do with this book. Whether you found the content insightful, the instructions clear, or if you have any suggestions for improvement (I WILL incorporate it into following books), your review will be appreciated.

By sharing your thoughts, you not only assist other seniors in making an informed choice but also support the author (that's me!). If you made it this far, I am offering the digital beta copy of our next book for all customers in hopes for some feedback.

Email me at:
JasonBrownPublishing@gmail.com

Thank you for considering this request. Your words can make a big difference, and together, we can make the Apple world even more accessible and enjoyable for everyone, everywhere!

Thank you,
Jason Brown

COMPANION GUIDE!

If you found our "Macbook Pro and Air for Seniors - A Simple Step-by-Step Guide" helpful, then you'll definitely want to check out our companion guides "iPhone 15 Guide - An Illustrated Step by Step Manual for Seniors".

This guide will help you navigate your iPhone with ease, from sending messages to capturing memories and everything in between.It is specifically designed to make technology accessible for beginners & seniors to confidently dive into the world of technology!

Are you ready to unlock more possibilities? Scan these QR codes on your iPhone and get your copy!

MAC AND OTHER APPLE CONNECTIVITY

AIRDROP ON YOUR MAC

Sharing Content with AirDrop on Your MacBook

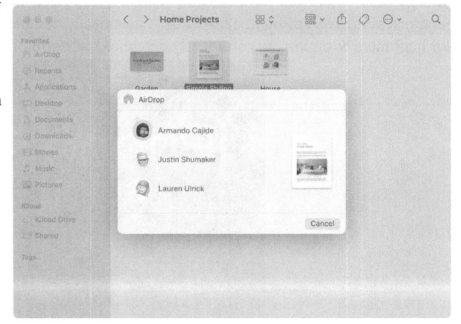

1. To share a file on your MacBook, first open it and click the "Share" button. For files found in the Finder, you can Control-click (or right-click) on the file, and then choose "Share" from the menu that appears.
2. Choose "AirDrop" from the options listed.
3. A list of nearby recipients will be displayed. Select the recipient to whom you want to send the file.

Alternatively, you can:

1. Open a Finder window and select "AirDrop" in the sidebar, or go to "Go > AirDrop" from the menu bar.
2. The AirDrop window will show nearby users. To send a file, drag it to the recipient you want to share with.

Receiving Files via AirDrop

If someone near you sends a file through AirDrop, you'll receive a notification or message in the AirDrop window.

1. Click "Accept" to download the file. It will be saved in your Downloads folder.
2. Troubleshooting AirDrop Connectivity Issues
3. Make sure both devices are within 30 feet of each other and have Wi-Fi and Bluetooth enabled.
4. On your MacBook, go to "Go > AirDrop" and adjust the "Allow me to be discovered by" settings. The device sending the file must also have similar settings.

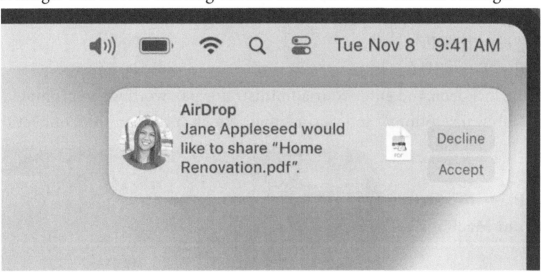

Troubleshooting AirDrop Connectivity Issues

If you're having trouble with AirDrop and can't seem to locate another device, follow these steps to resolve the issue:

- Proximity and Connectivity: Ensure that both devices are within range, within 9 meters (30 feet), and have both Wi-Fi and Bluetooth turned on.

- Visibility Settings: On your Mac, go to "Go > AirDrop" from the menu bar in the Finder.
- In the AirDrop window, check the option for "Allow me to be discovered by." For iPhones, iPads, and iPod touches, you can adjust a similar setting.
- If the "Contacts Only" setting is selected, you need to ensure that both devices are signed in to iCloud, and the sender's Apple ID information is saved in the receiver's Contacts app.

Software Updates: Make sure to keep your Mac and other devices updated with the latest software versions.

Firewall Settings: For macOS Ventura or later:

- Go to the Apple menu > System Settings.
- Select "Network" from the sidebar.
- Click on "Firewall" on the right-hand side.
- Click on the "Options" button.
- Ensure that "Block all incoming connections" is not selected.

For earlier versions of macOS

- Navigate to the Apple menu > System Preferences.
- Click "Security & Privacy."
- Go to the "Firewall" tab.
- Click the lock icon and enter your administrator password when prompted.
- Click "Firewall Options" and ensure that "Block all incoming connections" is not selected.

Using AirPlay to Stream Videos to Your MacBook

To stream from iPhone or iPad:

1. Both your mobile device and MacBook should be connected to the same Wi-Fi network.
2. Locate the video on your iPhone or iPad and tap the AirPlay icon.
3. Choose your MacBook from the list of available devices and press.

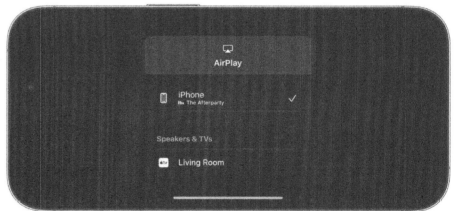

To stop streaming

1. Tap the AirPlay icon again and select your iPhone or iPad.

44

Automatic AirPlay Streaming

1. Go to Settings  on your iPhone or iPad.
2. Tap "General," then tap "AirPlay & Handoff" and select "Automatically AirPlay."
3. Choose from "Never," "Ask," or "Automatic" based on your preferences.

Mirroring iPhone or iPad Screen to MacBook

(Both devices must be on the same Wi-Fi network)

1. Open Control Center:
2. On iPhone X or later, or iPad with iPadOS 13 or later: Swipe down from the upper right corner.
3. On iPhone 8 or earlier, or with iOS 11 or earlier: Swipe up from the bottom.
4. Tap "Screen Mirroring" and choose your MacBook.
5. If prompted, enter the AirPlay passcode displayed on your MacBook screen.

To end the mirroring session:

- Open Control Center, tap "Screen Mirroring," and then tap "Stop Mirroring," or press the Menu button on your Apple TV remote.

This should provide you with detailed instructions for connecting your MacBook to other devices using AirDrop and AirPlay. Make sure to follow each step carefully!

APPLE PAY ON YOUR MAC AND OTHER DEVICES

Do you want to use Apple Pay on your Mac for online shopping? It's both convenient and secure. You can complete your transaction using your iPhone or Apple Watch.

Step 1: Activate Apple Pay on Your Mac

Open Settings ⚙ and select "Wallet & Apple Pay." Then, click the add button ➕ on the top right corner to add your credit or debit cards to Apple Pay.

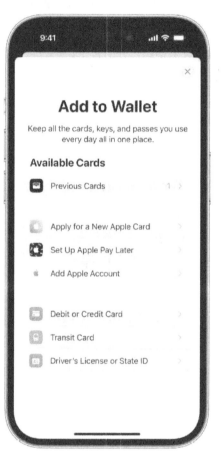

Step 2: Begin Your Online Shopping

Open your preferred web browser on your Mac and visit the online store where you'd like to shop. Add the items you want to your shopping cart and proceed to checkout.

Step 3: Opt for Apple Pay

At the checkout screen, click on the Apple Pay button to start the payment process.

Step 4: Approve the Transaction on Your iPhone or Apple Watch

After initiating payment on your Mac, a payment prompt will appear on your iPhone or Apple Watch if they are nearby and linked to the same account. On your iPhone, authenticate using Face ID, Touch ID, or your passcode. On your Apple Watch, confirm by double-clicking the side button.

Step 5: Complete Your Purchase

Once the payment is confirmed on your iPhone or Apple Watch, your Mac will notify you that the transaction is complete. You'll usually receive an email or an on-screen acknowledgment confirming your successful transaction.

HOTSPOT CONTINUITY

Are you also interested in sharing your iPhone or iPad's internet connection through Instant Hotspot? It's easy and secure. Here's how to do it:

Step 1: Configure Instant Hotspot

Ensure your iPhone or iPad has an activated cellular plan that includes Personal Hotspot. Sign in to iCloud using the same Apple ID on all devices you wish to connect. Enable Bluetooth and Wi-Fi on all participating devices.

Step 2: Connect to Instant Hotspot

To Connect from Your Mac

Click on the Wi-Fi symbol 📶 in the Control Center 🎚 or menu bar on your Mac. Locate and click on the name of your iPhone or iPad 🔗 offering the Personal Hotspot.

To Connect from Another iPhone or iPad

Open the "Settings" app ⚙️ and tap on "Wi-Fi." Find and tap on the name of the iPhone or iPad that is providing the Personal Hotspot.

By following these steps, you can smoothly conduct online shopping transactions via Apple Pay and securely share internet connections through Instant Hotspot.

CONTINUITY CAMERA

Continuity Camera is an innovative feature that allows you to seamlessly integrate your iPhone or iPad with your Mac to perform tasks such as scanning documents or taking pictures. Here's a step-by-step guide on how to use it.

Step 1: Open Compatible Apps on Your Mac

Finder	Notes
Keynote 8.2 or later	Numbers 5.2 or later
Mail	Pages 7.2 or later
Messages	TextEdit

To use the Continuity Camera, launch one of the following built-in apps on your Mac:

Step 2: Capture an Image

1. Open an app on your Mac that supports Continuity Camera.

2. Right-click where you want to insert the photo within the app window and select

"Insert from iPhone or iPad" > "Take Photo."

3. Your iPhone or iPad's Camera app will launch. Press the Shutter button ⚫ to capture the image.

4. Choose "Use Photo" on your iPhone or iPad, and the image will instantly appear in the app on your Mac.

Step 3: Scan Documents

1. Open a compatible app on your Mac.
2. Right-click where you want to insert the scan and select "Insert from iPhone or iPad" > "Scan Documents."
3. The Camera app will launch on your iPhone or iPad.
4. Align the document within the camera's view and wait for the scan to complete. If needed, press the Shutter button ⚫ to manually capture the scan.
5. Adjust the corners of the scanned image and tap "Keep Scan."
6. Press "Save" when done, and the scanned document will appear as a PDF on your Mac.

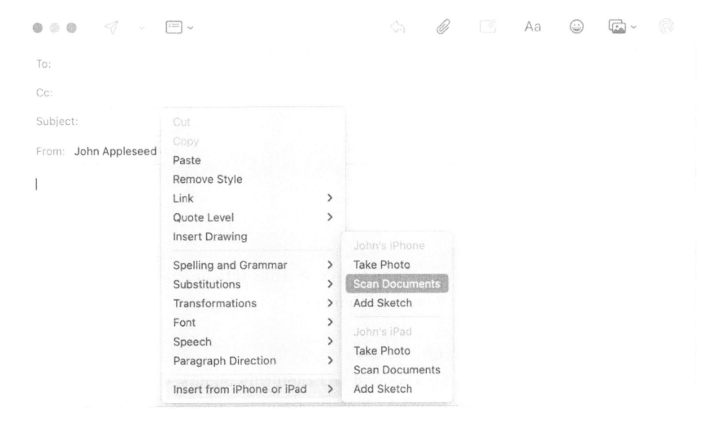

Use iPhone as a Webcam

Step 1: Position Your iPhone

1. Place your iPhone near your Mac.
2. Ensure it's securely mounted to avoid any movement.
3. The rear cameras should be facing you and unobstructed.
4. The iPhone can be placed in either landscape or portrait orientation.

Step 2: Select iPhone as Camera or Microphone

1. Open an app like FaceTime and, if not automatically selected, choose your iPhone from the camera menu.
2. To choose your iPhone as a microphone, go to Apple menu > System Preferences, click on Sound, and then choose your iPhone in the Input tab.

Step 3: Additional Features

macOS offers various additional features for video and audio, including Reactions, Presenter Overlay, and various camera and microphone modes.

Step 4: Pause or Disconnect

To pause, tap the Pause button on your iPhone.

To disconnect, tap the Disconnect button or move your iPhone out of your Mac's Bluetooth range.

Turning Off Continuity Camera

If you want to disable this feature, go to Settings on your iPhone, navigate to General > AirPlay & Handoff, and turn off Continuity Camera.

System Requirements for Continuity Camera

When using Continuity Camera for scanning and capturing photos, it is compatible with various devices and operating systems which meet certain specifications.Utilizing

- macOS Mojave or later	MacBook introduced in 2015 or later
MacBook Pro introduced in 2012 or later	MacBook Air introduced in 2012 or later
Mac mini introduced in 2012 or later	iMac introduced in 2012 or later
iMac Pro	Mac Pro introduced in 2013 or later
Mac Studio introduced in 2022 or later	iOS 12 or later
iPhone	iPad
iPod touch	
Additional Requirements	
- Both devices must have both Wi-Fi and Bluetooth turned on. - Both devices must be signed in with the same Apple ID using two-factor authentication. - Ensure your Mac is using the latest version of macOS.	

APPLE ID AND ICLOUD

iCloud is like a secure locker where you can keep your important files and photos. You get 5 GB of space for free. You can also buy more space if needed.

How to Sign In to iCloud on a Computer

1. Open an internet browser on your computer.
2. Visit the website iCloud.com.
3. To log in, you have two choices:

4. Type your Apple ID and password.
5. Or, if you're using Safari, you can use Face ID or Touch ID if your device has these features.
6. Sometimes, the website will ask you to prove it's really you. Just follow the steps on the screen.

What You Can Do on iCloud.com

- Use different apps like Mail, Contacts, and more.
- Click the app you want to use.
- Use the toolbar to switch between apps.
- How to Log Out of iCloud.com
- Click your profile picture at the top-right of the screen.
- Click "Sign Out."
- iCloud Drive: How to Use It on Your Mac or Windows Computer

On a Mac Computer:

For macOS 13.3 or Later

1. Click the Apple logo at the top-left of your screen.
2. Choose "System Preferences."
3. Click your name.
4. Click "iCloud."
5. Choose "iCloud Drive."
6. Make sure "Sync this Mac" is turned on.

For macOS 12 or Earlier:

1. Click the Apple logo and Choose "System Preferences."
2. Click "Apple ID." & Choose "iCloud Drive."

51

3. You can choose which folders to sync, like your Desktop and Documents.

To find your iCloud Drive files, open "Finder" and look in the sidebar.

On a Windows Computer:

1. Download and install iCloud for Windows.
2. Open the program and choose "iCloud Drive."
3. Click "Apply."
4. Accessing Desktop and Documents Files Through iCloud Drive

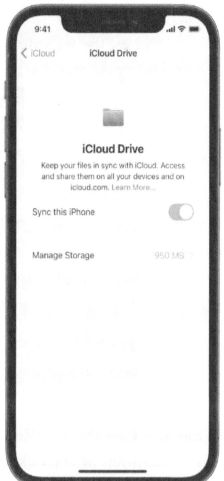

On a Mac:

1. Make sure iCloud Drive is turned on in "System Preferences."
2. Select "Desktop & Documents Folders."

On an iPhone or iPad:

1. Open the "Settings" app ⚙️.
2. Scroll to find your name and tap it. & Tap "iCloud."
3. Make sure "Sync this [device]" is on under "iCloud Drive."
4. To see your files, open the "Files" app on your device.

On iCloud.com:

1. Sign in and go to iCloud Drive.
2. Click on the folder you need.

Remember, deleting a file will remove it from all your devices.

How to Turn Off iCloud Features

1. Click the Apple logo 🍎 and Choose "System Preferences."
2. Click "Apple ID." * Choose "iCloud."
3. Next to iCloud Drive, click "Options."
4. Uncheck "Desktop & Documents Folders."
5. Click "Done."

This turns off the syncing feature, but your files will stay in iCloud.

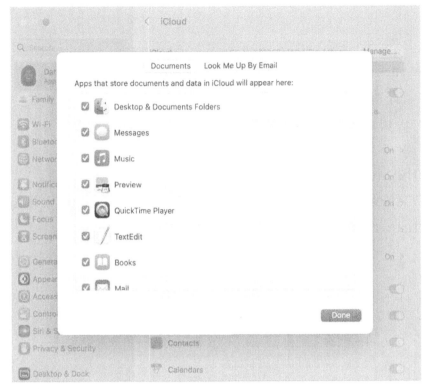

To turn off iCloud on your iPhone:

1. Open the settings app .

2. Press on your profile and scroll down to inactive press Access iCloud Data on the Web. If you turn off iCloud altogether, your files will be saved in a folder on your Mac. You can move them back to your local Desktop and Documents later if you wish.

HANDOFF TO ON YOUR MAC

Handoff is a convenient feature that lets you start a task on one Apple device and continue it on another without losing your progress. To use this feature, ensure that:

- Your Apple devices meet the Continuity system requirements.

- Wi-Fi and Bluetooth are turned on for all your devices.
- You are signed in with the same Apple ID on every device you want to use with Handoff.

To enable or disable Handoff, follow these steps:

On your Mac:
1. Click the Apple logo at the top-left corner of your screen.
2. Choose "System Preferences."
3. Click "General" from the list on the side.
4. Look for the section that says "Allow Handoff between this Mac and your iCloud devices." Here, you can turn the feature on or off.

On your iPhone or iPad:
1. Open the "Settings" app .
2. Scroll down and tap "General."
3. Tap "AirPlay & Handoff."
4. Here you can turn Handoff on or off.

On your Apple Watch:
1. Open the Apple Watch app on your iPhone.
2. Go to "My Watch." & Tap "General."
3. Here, you can turn "Enable Handoff" on or off.

To use Handoff to switch between devices, follow these steps:

Click to continue what you were doing on your iPhone.

From your Mac to an iPhone or iPad:

When using an app on your Mac, look for its Handoff icon to appear on your iPhone or iPad. Tap that icon to continue what you were doing on your Mac.

From an iPhone, iPad, or Apple Watch to your Mac:

When using an app on your iPhone, iPad, or Apple Watch, look for its Handoff icon to appear on your Mac's Dock. Click on that icon to pick up where you left off.

Quick Tip:

You can use the "Command-Tab" keys on your Mac keyboard to quickly switch to the app showing the Handoff icon.

USING UNIVERSAL CLIPBOARD ACROSS APPLE DEVICES

Universal Clipboard and Universal Control are remarkable features that allow seamless interactions between your Apple devices.

Requirements and Setup

- Your devices should meet the Continuity system requirements.
- Wi-Fi, Bluetooth, and Handoff must be enabled in System Settings on your Mac and in the Settings app on iOS and iPadOS devices.
- Log in with the same Apple ID on all devices.

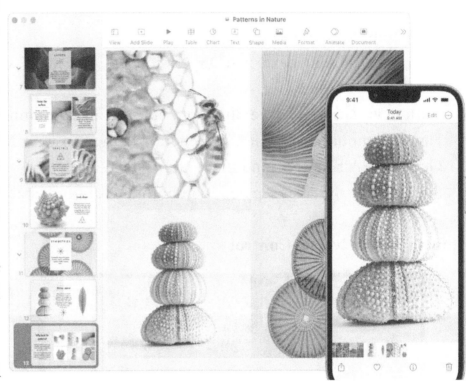

How to Use Universal Clipboard

Copying Content:

- Highlight the content you want to copy.
- Perform the standard copy action (e.g., press Command-C on your Mac).

Pasting Content:

- Place the cursor where you want to paste the content.
- Perform the standard paste action (e.g., double-tap and select "Paste" on your iPad).

Types of Content:

- Text
- Images
- Photos

- Videos
- Files

You can transfer these between any apps that support copy and paste on your devices.

Universal Control

This feature allows you to control multiple devices using a single keyboard, mouse, or trackpad.

Requirements and Setup

- Your Mac should have macOS version 12.3 or later, and your iPad should run on iPadOS 15.4 or later.
- Both devices should have Bluetooth enabled and be connected to Wi-Fi.
- Handoff should be enabled in General settings on your MacBook and under Settings > General > AirPlay & Handoff on your iPad.
- Sign in with the same Apple ID on both devices and enable two-factor authentication.

How to Use Universal Control

Connecting Devices:

1. Click on Control Center in your Mac's menu bar.
2. Select "Screen Mirroring."
3. Under "Link Keyboard and Mouse," pick a device to connect.

Navigating Between Screens:

- Move the mouse pointer to the edge of your Mac screen closest to your iPad.
- Pause briefly and continue moving past the edge. A border will appear on the iPad,

indicating connection.

Drag and Drop:

Highlight what you want to transfer.

Drag it to its destination on the other device.

Sharing a Keyboard:

- Position the pointer in a text input field on either device.
- Begin typing; the text will appear where the pointer is active.

Universal Control enriches your productivity, allowing you to work seamlessly between your Mac and iPad.

PHONE CALL AND TEXT FROM YOUR MAC

To speak with friends and family through video or audio, FaceTime on your Mac is quite handy.

Initiating a FaceTime Call

1. Open your Mac's FaceTime application 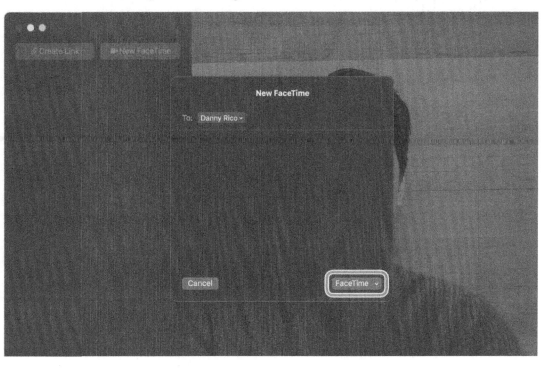 .
2. Click "Start New FaceTime."
3. Type in the contact details of the person you wish to call.
4. Choose either the Video or Audio option to begin the call. Alternatively, click the arrow ⌄ next to it and choose FaceTime Audio for an audio call. If you can't see these options, click either the Video or Audio button.

Ending a Call

Click the red button labeled "End" to exit the call.

Managing Group Calls

- The person speaking will appear in a larger tile.
- Click on any tile to see who it is. Double-click to enlarge it.

Adding More People to the Call

- Click the sidebar button.
- Click the add button and type in the contact details of the new person.
- Click "Ring" to call them.

Using FaceTime Links

- Generate a FaceTime link by clicking on the sharing menu.
- Double-click the link to begin the call.
- Participants who click the link need to be allowed into the call.

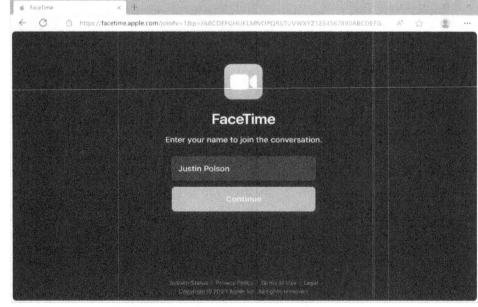

- To let a participant join the call, click the tick next to their name.

- If you want to decline a participant's request to join the call, click the decline button 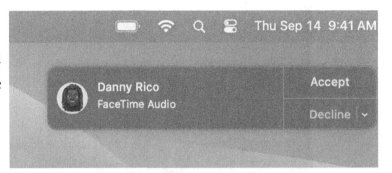 next to their name.
- If you need to remove a participant from the call within 30 seconds of them joining, click the remove button ⊗.

Answering a Call

- Click "Accept" on the notification to take the incoming FaceTime call.

Transferring a Call to Another Device

- Click "Join" or "Switch" on the device you want to move the call to.

Sending Texts from Your Mac

BBefore you can send messages from your Mac, you need to set up the connection from your phone to Laptop. To do this:

When the message bubbles are green, it means they were sent as SMS text messages.

1. Open the "Settings" app 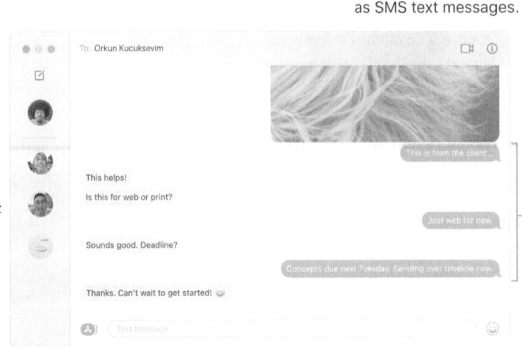 on your iPhone and select "Messages."
2. Go to "Text Message Forwarding."
3. Activate your Mac from the list.

UNLOCKING YOUR MAC USING YOUR APPLE WATCH

Initial Setup

1. Sign in on your Apple Watch and Mac with the same Apple ID.
2. Enable two-factor authentication.
3. Open "System Preferences" on your Mac and click on "Touch ID & Password" .
4. Activate the Apple Watch unlock settings.

Unlocking Your Mac

5. Wake up your Mac by opening the lid or pressing a key, and your Apple Watch will automatically unlock it for you.

Approving Tasks on Your Mac with Your Apple Watch

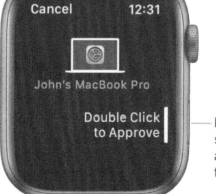

- Double-click the side button on your Apple Watch to authenticate tasks on your Mac.
- Use this to approve installations, view passwords, and more.

Double-click the side button to approve requests from your Mac.

AIRPRINT

How to Use AirPrint on Your Mac and Print Documents or Photos Wirelessly

Confirm that your printer is compatible with AirPrint (only specific printers can do this).

1. Open the application that contains the document or photo you want to print.
2. Click on the "File" menu in the top-left corner, then choose "Print." Alternatively, you can also press the Command-P keys together.
3. A window titled "Print" will open. Click where it says "Printer."
4. A list of "Nearby Printers" will appear. Choose your printer from this list.

What to Do If Your Printer Isn't Listed

If your printer doesn't appear in the list, don't worry. Here are some steps to troubleshoot:

1. Check that your printer and your MacBook are both connected to the same Wi-Fi network.

2. If they are on the same network but your printer still isn't showing up, you can add it manually by doing the following:

   A. Open "System Preferences" from your Mac's Dock or Apple menu.
   B. Click on "Printers & Scanners" listed on the left-hand side.
   C. On the right-hand side, click on "Add Printer, Scanner, or Fax."
   D. As a last resort, you might need to connect your printer to your Mac with a USB cable. If your Mac doesn't have a USB port, you may require an adapter.

APPS

Enjoy Apple's pre-installed apps and in-app functionalities for entertainment, seamless connections, and enhanced productivity.

App Store

Included Apps

Icon/App name	Icon/App name	Icon/App name
App Store	Books	Calendar
FaceTime	Find My	Freeform
GarageBand	Home	iMovie
Keynote	Mail	Maps
Messages	Music	News
Notes	Numbers	Pages
Photos	Podcasts	Preview
Reminders	Safari	Shortcuts
Stocks	TV	Voice Memos

Apart from the apps mentioned in the table on the previous page, your Mac also has other apps and utilities that could be useful. These include Calculator ▦ Chess ▦ Clock 🕐 , Contacts ⬤ , TextEdit ▱ , Weather ☁ , and many more. To find these additional apps, follow these steps:

1. Open your Applications folder. You can do this by clicking on the desktop or using Finder 🙂 from your Dock, then selecting "Go" from the menu bar and choosing "Applications."

2. Inside the Applications folder, you'll find a wide range of apps and utilities, some of which may not be featured in the table mentioned earlier.

3. If you want to explore a complete list of all the apps and utilities installed on your Mac, refer to the macOS User Guide for a detailed inventory.

4. Additionally, if you're looking for more apps to enhance your Mac's capabilities, you can visit the App Store. To access the App Store, click on its icon 🅰 in your Dock. The App Store offers a vast selection of apps to fulfill almost any task you have in mind.

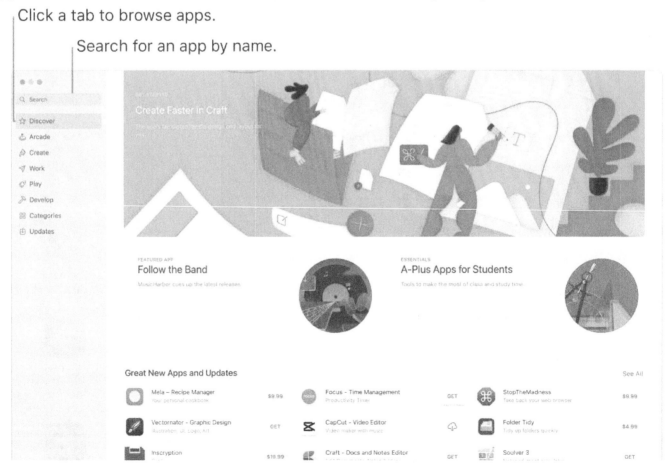

The next section explores each aspect of the app store and their functions

Finding Apps

To look for a specific app, simply type its name into the search bar and press the Return key. Once you download an app, it will automatically show up in your Launchpad for quick access.

Using Siri

If you're comfortable with voice commands, you can ask Siri to find apps for you. Just say something like, "Siri, find apps for cooking."

Signing In

To get free apps, you'll need to sign in using your Apple ID. You'll find the "Sign In" option at the bottom of the App Store sidebar. If you don't have an Apple ID, you can create one by clicking "Create Apple ID."

iPhone and iPad Apps

Many apps that you've purchased or downloaded on your iPhone or iPad are also available on your Mac. You can search for them in the App Store.

Apple Arcade

For gaming enthusiasts, Apple Arcade offers a wide range of games. Click on the Arcade tab to explore. These games will also appear in your Launchpad for quick access.

Game Capture

You can capture short 15-second videos of your gameplay using supported game controllers by pressing the share button.

Keeping Apps Updated

To keep your apps current, look at the App Store icon in your Dock. If it has a badge, that means updates are available. Click on the icon

You have available updates.

and then choose "Updates" from the sidebar.

Touch Bar Features

If your 13-inch MacBook has a Touch Bar, you can use it to navigate the App Store more easily.

BOOKS

If you want to buy books and audiobooks using the Books app 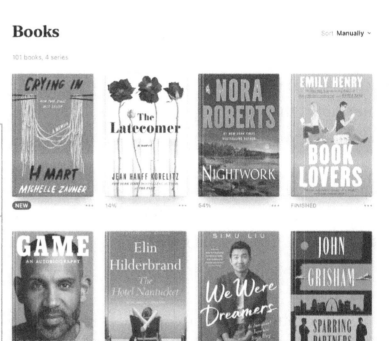 on your Mac, it's a piece of cake.

The Books app on your Mac is a one-stop library for all your reading needs - books or audiobooks. You can purchase and download new titles, and it keeps track of your reading history, bookmarks, and notes. You can set daily reading goals to motivate yourself and sync your library across multiple devices using your Apple ID. The app also provides advanced features like Night mode for comfortable reading in low light. Whether you're a casual reader or an avid bookworm, the Books app makes managing your reading experience both convenient and enjoyable.

Type what you're looking for.

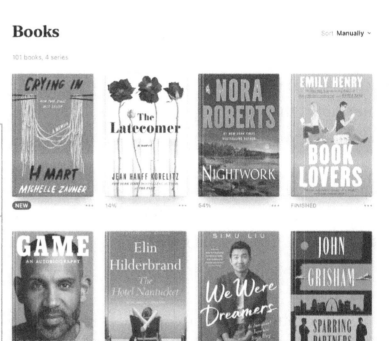

View your books and lists.

How to Search for Books or Audiobooks

1. Open the Books app on your Mac.
2. Click in the search box at the top.
3. Type what you're looking for—this could be the book title, the author, or even the genre.
4. As you type, suggestions will appear. You can click on one or press Return to search.
5. To narrow down your search, you can use the "Filter by" options or click "All" to see every result.

Exploring the Book and Audiobook Stores

In the Books app, you'll see options for the Book Store and Audiobook Store on the side menu.

1. To explore, either scroll down or click on "Browse Sections" located at the top-right.

2. You can choose a category like "For You," "Top Charts," or a specific genre like "History."
3. Setting Your Reading Goals
4. To keep track of your reading, set a daily reading goal. The default goal is 5 minutes per day.
5. To change this, click the "Adjust Goal" button � in the "Reading Goals" section, found under "Reading Now."

Adding Bookmarks and Notes

1. While reading, hover your mouse near the top of the screen to reveal additional options.
2. Click the "Add Bookmark" button 🔖 mark a page. To unmark it, click the bookmark again ▤ .
3. To find a bookmark, hover at the top, click the "Show Bookmarks" button 🔖 , and choose the one you want.
4. You can also highlight text and add notes. To see them later, click the "Notes and Highlights" button.

Syncing Between Devices

All your purchases, bookmarks, and notes will be available on any Apple device signed in with your Apple ID.

How to Buy or Download Books

1. Go to the Book Store, found in the sidebar of the Books app 📖 .
2. Find a book you like and click its price or the "Get" button to download it.
3. To save for later, click "Want to Read." This adds it to a special collection in your library.
4. Some books offer a "Sample" button. Click it to read a preview. The sample is saved under "My Samples."

Night Reading Mode

If you prefer reading in darker settings, switch to Night theme. Go to View > Theme, and then choose "Night." Note that some books may not support this theme.

CALENDAR

The Calendar app on your Mac is a versatile tool designed to manage your time and schedules effectively. It allows you to create and organize events, personalize your calendars with different colors, and even add holiday calendars to keep track of special dates. The app also integrates with the Focus feature to help you filter which calendars are visible at specific times. You can share calendars with others and synchronize them across all your Apple devices.

Whether for personal or professional use, the Calendar app helps you stay organized and proactive about your time management.

Creating Events
Click the "Add" button ╬ or double-click on any day to initiate a new event.

To invite participants, double-click on the created event, and in the "Add Invitees" section, type their email addresses.
The app will notify you about their responses.

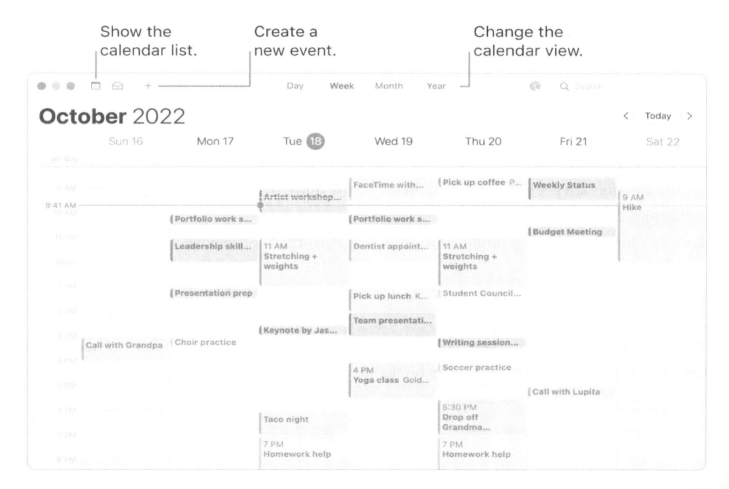

Customizing Calendars

You can establish separate calendars for various aspects of your life. Go to File > New Calendar to create a new one. Control-click the calendar name to assign it a color of your choice.

Adding Holiday Calendars:

To incorporate holiday calendars from across the globe, go to File > New Holiday Calendar.
Select the desired holiday calendar to add it to your list.

Filtering Calendars with Focus:

Navigate to Apple Menu > System Preferences, and then click on "Focus" in the sidebar. Choose the Focus you want to use, click the right arrow, and then select "Add Filter" under Focus Filters.

Sharing Calendars:

Sign in to iCloud to sync your calendars across all your Apple devices using the same Apple ID.
You can also share your calendars with other iCloud users.

Using the Touch Bar (for MacBook Pro users):

Tap the "Today" button on the Touch Bar to quickly view or edit the events of the day.
Use the slider to navigate through months, either past or future.
For a selected event, use the Touch Bar to modify the calendar, view event specifics, adjust the time or location, and manage invitees.

By following these guidelines, you'll find it much easier to manage your appointments, keep track of special dates, and coordinate schedules with others.

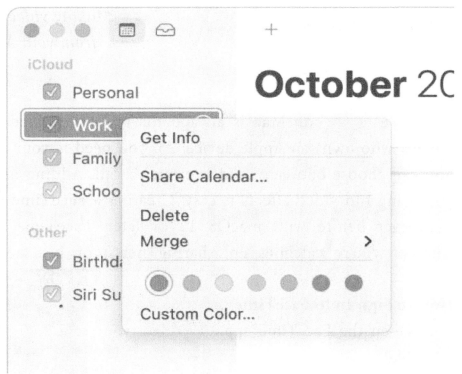

FACETIME

Making video, audio, and group calls directly from your Mac is simple, all with just a few simple steps.

FaceTime 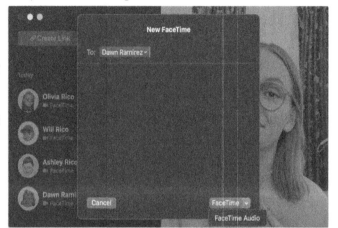 on Mac is an app for real-time video and audio conversations with anyone who owns an Apple device. All you need is your Apple ID to start making calls. You can choose between a video or audio call. Adding more people to the conversation and using fun video effects is easy. Creating a FaceTime link to invite others is simpler than ever before with macOS 12 or later. FaceTime makes connections enjoyable, whether you're catching up, sharing news, or just needing to see a familiar face.

How to Sign In to FaceTime

1. Open the FaceTime app on your Mac.
2. Enter your Apple ID and password in the FaceTime window.
3. Click "Next."

How to Make a Call

1. Click the arrow or "New FaceTime" button.
2. Enter the phone number, email address, or name of the person you want to call.
3. Click "FaceTime" for a video call or "FaceTime Audio" for an audio-only call.

How to Accept or Decline Calls

1. Click "Answer" to accept the call immediately.
2. Click to accept an audio-only call.
3. Click "Decline" to decline the call.
4. Alternatively, message the caller or set a remi

How to Add People to a Call

1. Click the "Sidebar" button.
2. Click the plus button next to "Add People" for a video call.

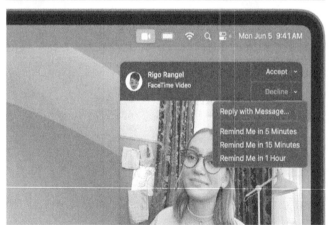
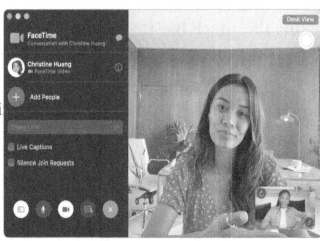

3. For an audio-only call, click the "Audio" button in the menu bar, then the ⌄ arrow in the window that appears, and then "Add."

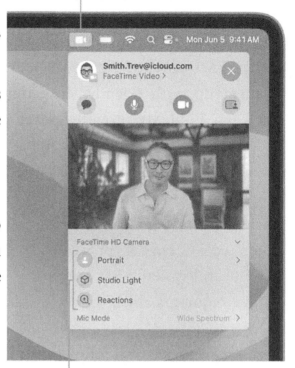

Appears when you're in a FaceTime call.

Depending on your Mac, you can adjust some or all of these video effects.

How to Use Video Effects

1. During a FaceTime video call, click the "Video" button in the menu bar.
2. Choose from available video effects, such as reactions, blur your background, turn on Centre Stage, and more.

How to Create a FaceTime Link

- - If you have macOS 12 or later, sign in to your Apple ID and click "Create Link" in the FaceTime app to generate a link for the FaceTime call.

How to Start a Call from a FaceTime Link

Double-click the FaceTime call link or find it in the list of recent calls in the "Upcoming" section.
Click the "Video" button and then "Join" to start the call.

How to Let Callers Join the FaceTime Call

1. As the originator of the FaceTime link, you can allow others to join the call immediately.
2. When a new caller is waiting, you'll see a badge on the "Sidebar" button.
3. Click the "Sidebar" button and choose to "Allow the caller to join the call" or "Don't allow the caller to join the call."

How to Delete a FaceTime Link

1. Check the list of callers for the call made with a FaceTime link.
2. Click the "Info" button and select "Delete Link."

FIND MY APP

Find My is a helpful app that enables you to locate your friends, family, and Apple devices.

The Find My app 🔘 is a reliable companion for staying connected with important people and protecting your Apple devices and personal belongings. Whether you're planning to meet up with friends, ensuring you don't forget your MacBook, or searching for lost keys, Find My provides peace of mind. You can use it to share your location with selected people, set up alerts for arriving or leaving certain places, and secure your lost devices by remotely locking or erasing them. It's an essential tool for anyone looking to stay connected with their world and safeguard their Apple ecosystem. It proves to be useful in daily life and critical moments alike.

Here are some easy-to-follow tips to help you with sharing your location and finding your lost devices:

To share your location with friends and family

1. Go to the People list and click "Share My Location".
2. Choose how long you want to share your live location.
3. Stop sharing whenever you want.
4. Follow a friend to see their location on a map and get directions to their whereabouts.

To get notified when you arrive at or leave a specific location

1. Configure location alerts on your iPhone, iPad, or iPod touch.
2. Get notifications when your friends arrive or leave particular places.
3. Find all location notifications about yourself in one place by clicking "Me" in the People list and scrolling to "Notifications About You."

To avoid leaving your devices behind

1. Set up separation alerts on your iPhone, iPad, or iPod touch.
2. Click the Info icon for that device and select "Notify When Left Behind."
3. Follow the onscreen instructions to complete the setup.

To locate and protect your lost devices

1. Use Find My to locate your lost devices, such as your Mac, iPhone, or AirPods.
2. Play a sound on the device to help you find it.
3. Mark it as lost to prevent others from accessing your personal information.
4. Erase it remotely for added security.

To find your everyday items

1. Register an AirTag and compatible third-party items to your Apple ID.
2. Find your items like your keychain by using Find My on your Mac.
3. Activate Lost Mode for an item, including a custom message and contact number for recovery.

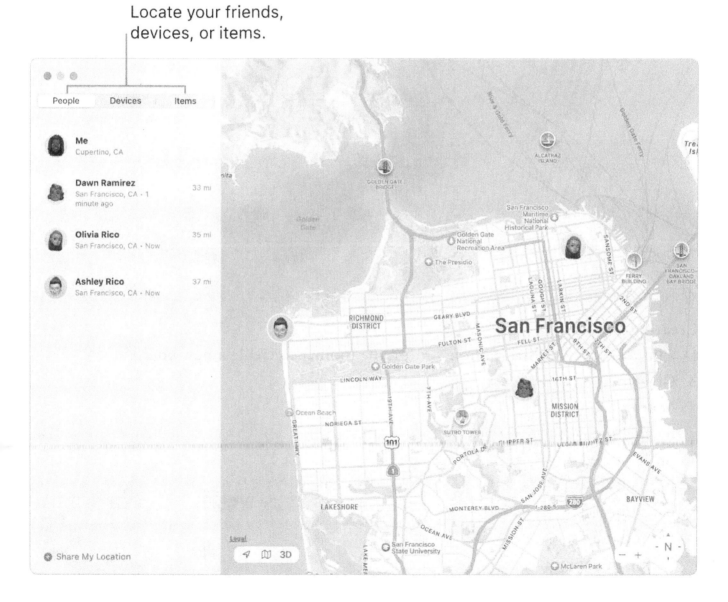

Locate your friends, devices, or items.

FREE FORM

Unleash collaborative creativity and organize your thoughts effortlessly on macOS Ventura 13.1, where every idea finds its place on your digital canvas.

Freeform  is a versatile app that helps you create and organize boards for various purposes while collaborating with others on macOS Ventura 13.1 or later. Whether you're planning a project, brainstorming ideas, or working with a team, the Freeform app  can help you achieve your goals.

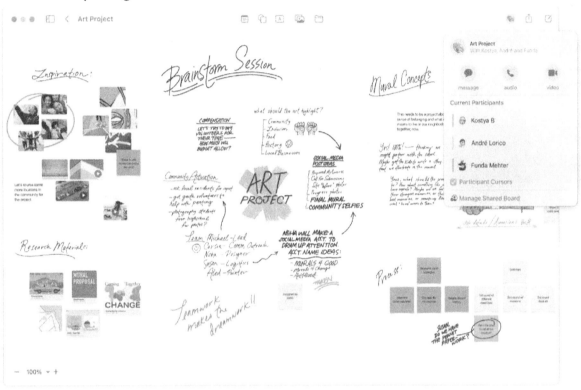

Creating a Board

1. Click the "New Board" button on the toolbar to create a new board.

2. Give your board a name by clicking on "Untitled" in the title bar's top-left corner and typing in your desired title. The boards get saved automatically.

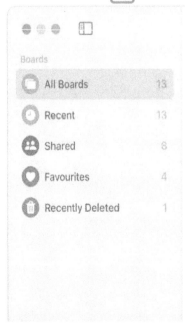

Adding Content

1. Use the toolbar to add various elements to your board, such as text , sticky notes pictures , hyperlinks, and files.
2. You can also drag and drop items from other applications directly onto your board.

Organizing Your Board

1. Freeform offers tools to help you arrange and manage board items. You can move, resize, group, or align items as you see fit.
2. You can enable a grid view or use alignment guides for precise placement of items.

Collaboration

1. Collaborate in real-time by inviting others to join your board.
2. To send invites, click the share icon on the toolbar, select "Collaborate," and choose your preferred method: Messages, Mail, or a copied link.

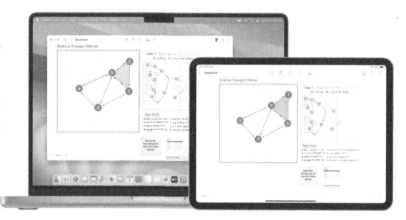

Export as a PDF

1. If you want to create a PDF version of your board, go to "File" and select "Export PDF."

Syncing Across Devices

1. Freeform boards are synced across all compatible devices, ensuring uniform access and collaboration.
2. If you encounter syncing issues, activate Freeform in your iCloud Settings.

Compatibility

Freeform is compatible with iOS 16.2 and iPadOS 16.2 or later, allowing for seamless interaction across different Apple devices.

HOME

The Home app 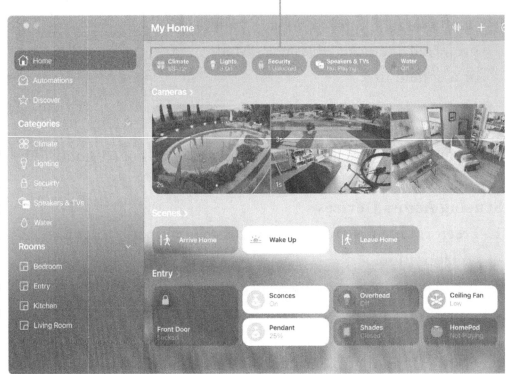 on your Mac is a centralized control system for all your smart home needs. It's the perfect tool for anyone looking to enhance their home's safety, convenience, and ambiance. Whether you're dimming the lights for a movie night, adjusting the temperature, or checking in on your home while away, the Home app makes it all possible with just a few clicks or a quick word with Siri. Use it to bring the power of home automation to your fingertips, creating a living space that's not only smart but intuitively adapts to your lifestyle and needs.

Safely manage your home accessories with your Mac

Use your Mac to securely control your smart home devices through Siri and the Home app. This section will guide you on leveraging the Home app to command your home accessories and set up scenes using Siri's voice controls.

Understanding the Home App

On your Mac, the Home app provides a unified dashboard of your smart home setup. It displays all connected cameras, scene configurations, and HomeKit-enabled devices by room, offering a secure way to oversee items like lights and thermostats.

Accessory categories

Managing Accessories

Interacting with your home devices is straightforward with the Home app's icon-based tiles. Easily switch lights on or off, secure doors, adjust window shades, and control other settings. Fine-tuning brightness and temperature settings is also simple.

Click an accessory to control it.

Navigating Categories

The Home app organizes accessories into categories such as Lights, Climate, Security, Speakers & TVs, and Water. Each category is sorted by room for quick access, complete with up-to-date status reports.

Setting Up Scenes

With the Home app, you can create scenes that coordinate multiple accessories with one command. Set a "Good Night" scene to power down lights, draw the shades, and lock up for the evening with a single action.

Monitoring Home Security

The app integrates with your HomeKit Secure Video-enabled cameras, allowing you to securely record and monitor your home. View up to nine camera feeds simultaneously on the Home tab, all with secure encryption.

Using Adaptive Lighting

The adaptive lighting feature lets you configure smart lights to alter their color temperature during the day, promoting a comfortable and productive environment.

Voice Commands with Siri

You can also use Siri to control your home, here are some examples of what you can ask it.

Light Control:
- "Turn on the lights."
- "Dim the lights," followed by specifying the brightness, such as "Set brightness to 55 percent."

Checking Light Status:
- "Is the hallway light on?"

Thermostat Control:
- "Set the temperature to 20 degrees."

Garage Door Control:
- "Close the garage door."

Room and Scene Control:(If you've set up specific rooms or scenes, use commands)
- "I'm home" or "I'm leaving."
- "Turn down the kitchen lights."
- "Turn on the fan in the office."

MAIL

The Mail application ✉ on your Mac is a comprehensive email client that consolidates various email services into one streamlined interface. It's designed for convenience, allowing you to manage multiple accounts from providers such as iCloud, Gmail, Yahoo, and others. With features like smart search, message scheduling, and privacy protection, it caters to efficiency and security in your digital communication.

The integration of Siri for voice-controlled email drafting, the ability to undo sending emails, and the "Hide My Email" function for iCloud+ users, enhance the overall user experience. Whether you're looking to maintain a clean inbox, ensure your privacy, or simply make email management more accessible, the Mail application ✉ on your Mac integrates all your email services like iCloud, Gmail, Yahoo, and others into one interface for streamlined email management.

Unified Email Accounts:

Easily set up and view multiple email accounts within the Mail app to centralize your email communication. To add a new account, simply navigate to Mail > Add Account.

Effective Message Management:

Manage your inbox by blocking specific senders, muting active threads, or unsubscribing from newsletters right within the app.

Email Scheduling:

Choose the ideal time to send your emails by using the send later feature available in the dropdown menu next to the Send button.

Intelligent Search:

The app's smart search not only corrects your spelling errors but also recommends synonyms and displays an enhanced view of shared content within emails, simplifying your search process. You can search for any email using the magnifying glass 🔍 on the top right of your screen, seen in the picture on the next page.

Undo Send Option:

Made a mistake? You have 10 seconds or a customizable duration to retract an email after sending, adjustable via Mail Settings > Composing.

Magnifying Glass

Click to Undo Send.

Organizational Alerts:

Mail alerts you when you miss adding an attachment or a recipient. It also helps you keep track of unsent messages by bringing them to the forefront of your inbox for follow-up.

Translation Tools:

Quickly translate highlighted text by right-clicking and choosing "Translate." Languages can be downloaded for offline use through Apple Menu > System Settings, then selecting General.

Reminders:

Set reminders for emails you've read but haven't yet responded to by right-clicking the message and selecting "Remind Me."

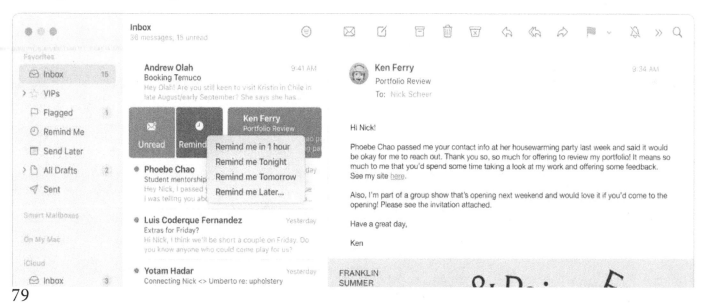

Integration with Events and Contacts:

Directly add new contacts or calendar events from email contents to your Contacts or Calendar with a simple click.

Privacy Measures:

Activate Privacy Protection in Mail Settings > Privacy to mask your IP address and prevent senders from knowing if you've opened their email.

Siri for Email:

Utilize Siri to quickly compose and send emails. Just instruct Siri with commands like, "Email [contact name] about [subject]."

Hide My Email:

For those with iCloud+, use the Hide My Email feature to create anonymous email addresses that forward to your inbox, safeguarding your actual email address.

Personal Touches:

Add a personal flair to your emails with emojis, photos, or sketches. Insert images directly or use your iPhone or iPad to capture new ones with the Continuity Camera feature.

Focused Writing in Full Screen:

When you write in full screen, the Mail app opens a new message in Split View, allowing you to keep other emails in sight, facilitating easy reference.

This suite of features in the Mail app not only enhances privacy and search capabilities but also streamlines the management and composition of emails, all from the convenience of your Mac.

MAPS

The Maps application on your Mac serves as your personal travel guide, helping you discover new places and navigate with ease. It's a versatile tool that not only offers turn-by-turn directions but also allows you to explore destinations before you even set foot

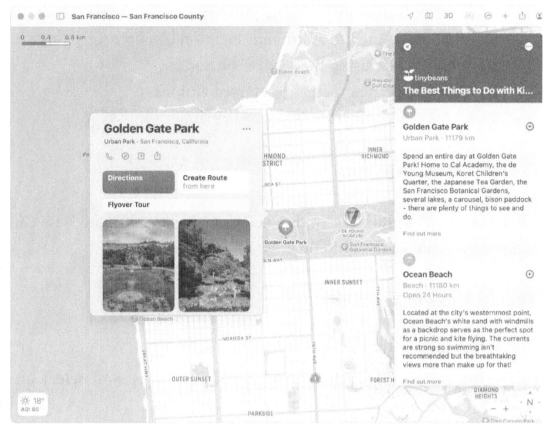

there. With Guides curated by experts and a Look Around feature that provides street-level imagery, you can plan your trip, get familiar with new locales, or simply explore from the comfort of your home. Whether you're plotting a road trip with multiple stops or looking to find the best local eats, Maps turns your Mac into a window to the world.

Open your Apple Maps to embark on a journey of discovery. Just type in what you're interested in the search box to find a curated Guide under "Favorites," or browse the full collection by selecting "Explore More Guides."

Finding and Using Guides

Open the Maps app and click on the search field.

Choose from the suggested Guides under "Guides We Love," or click on "See All" to view more options.

You can also search for a specific term and select a Guide from the results.

Within a Guide, you can:

- Browse locations by scrolling.
- Save a Guide by clicking the "More" button and selecting or "Add to My

Guides."

- Add a place to your Guide or create a new one if needed.
- View other Guides by the same publisher or visit their website.
- Find Guides related to a different location by exploring "Editors' Picks." using ⊙
- Share any Guide using the "Share" button ⬆.
- Engage with related media in selected Guides.
- Close the Guide when finished by pressing ⊗.

Creating Your Own Guide

Click the "New" button ✛ in the toolbar and select "Create New Guide."
Name your Guide and tap Return.

Adding Places to Your Guide

Select a location on the map.
In the information card that appears, click "Add" ⊞ and select one of your Guides, or create a new one.

Managing Your Guides

- To rename a Guide:
  » Right-click on the Guide, select "Edit Guide," and type in the new title.
- To change the Guide's cover image:
  » Right-click on the Guide, choose "Edit Guide," then select "Change Key Photo."
- To remove a Guide:
  » Right-click on the desired Guide and select "Delete Guide" from the menu.
- To take out a location from the Guide:
  » Hover over the Guide, click the small arrow, right-click on the location, and select "Remove from Guide."
- To adjust the order of the entries:
  » Hover over the Guide, click the small arrow, select the "Sort Order" button, and then pick the preferred sorting criterion - by Name, Distance, or Date Added.
- To transfer a location to a different Guide:
  » Hover over the Guide, click the small arrow, right-click on the location, select "Move to," and then choose the Guide you want to move the location to.

Sharing Your Guides

Within "My Guides," control-click a Guide and pick a sharing option. If your Guides aren't showing, tap the arrow ⟩.

Getting Directions

Maps offer detailed directions for driving, walking, public transit, and cycling. You can also plan routes with multiple stops for driving and easily send these directions to your iPhone, iPad, or Apple Watch for convenience when you're on the move.

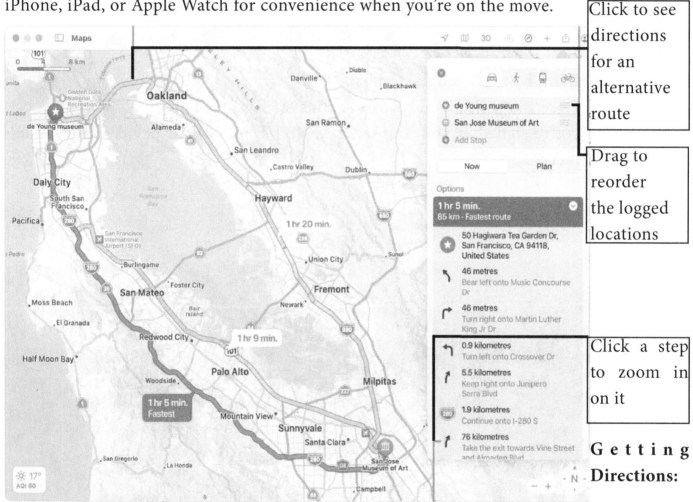

Click to see directions for an alternative route

Drag to reorder the logged locations

Click a step to zoom in on it

Getting Directions:

Getting Directions with Multiple Stops During a Drive:
1. Launch the Maps application 🅰 on your Mac.
2. Click the "Directions" button ↪ located in the toolbar.
3. Type in your initial location and final destination.
4. Select the "Drive" option 🚗.
5. To include additional stops, click "Add stop," then you can either pick a place from recent searches or look up a new one and click on the result.
   - If you need to, you can reorder the stops by dragging ☰, change any details, or remove a stop ⌄.

Accessing Directions on Your iPhone or iPad Automatically:

To open the route you've found on your Mac in the Maps app on your iPhone or iPad:

Open the Maps app  on your iPhone or iPad.
In the search overview, scroll to "Recent" and tap on the desired route.

Sending Directions to Your iPhone, iPad, or Apple Watch:

1. On your Mac's Maps app, click a location and then "Directions."
2. Adjust the route if necessary.
3. Click the "Share" button on the toolbar.
4. Select the device you wish to send the directions to.
- Make sure you're signed in with the same Apple ID on all your devices for seamless sharing and access.

Exploring Maps in Look Around Mode on Mac:

1. Open the Maps app on your Mac.
2. Input an address, intersection, landmark, or business in the search field.
3. If "Look Around" is available, click on it beneath the location in the search results,

choose a spot, then click the "Look Around" button ⚇ in the toolbar, or click on the image marked with the "Look Around" button at the bottom left of the information card.

When using Look Around:

- To Pan: Drag the image left or right.
- To Move Forward: Click ahead in the Look Around view.
- To Zoom In or Out: Pinch your fingers apart to zoom in, or pinch them together to zoom out.
- To View a Different Area: Click on another spot on the map.
- For Full Screen: Click the "Enter Full Screen" button ⤢. To leave, click "Exit Full Screen" ⤡.
- To Exit Look Around: Click the "Close" button ⊗ when finished.

MESSAGES

The Messages app ⬤ on Mac is a versatile communication tool that enables users to send text, photos, videos, and audio messages from their computer. It is integrated with the Apple ecosystem, offering a seamless messaging experience that syncs with your iPhone and iPad via iCloud. People use Messages to stay connected with friends and family, share media, and continue conversations across devices without interruption.

If you're new to using Messages on your Mac, here's how to get started:

- Starting the Messages application: Simply locate the Messages app ⬤ on your Mac and open it.
- Creating a new message: To begin a new message, click the "Compose" button 📝 located in the upper-right section or use the Touch Bar if your Mac model supports it.
- Selecting a recipient: In the "To" field, type the recipient's name, email, or phone number. The Messages app will display suggestions from your contacts or past conversations as you type. You can also click the "Add" button next to the "To" field, pick someone from your contacts, and then click their email or phone number.
- Writing your message: At the bottom of the window, you'll find a field where you can type your message. You can take advantage of typing suggestions if available.
- Sending your message: To dispatch your message, either press the "Return" key on your keyboard or click the "Send" button.
- Enhancing your messages: The Messages app includes features like Tapbacks, the ability to attach photos, videos, stickers, audio messages, and use message effects to add flair to your conversations.

How to Use Messages ⬤ on Your Mac:

Creating a New Message:

To begin a new message, click the "Compose" button 📝 , situated in the upper-right section, or use the Touch Bar if your Mac model is equipped with it.

Selecting a Recipient:

In the "To" field, type the recipient's name, email, or phone number. The Messages app will display suggestions from your Contacts or past conversations as you type.

You can also click the "Add" button ⊕ next to the "To" field, pick someone from your contacts, and then click their email or phone number.

Writing Your Message:

At the bottom of the window, you'll find a field where you can type your message. If available, you can take advantage of typing suggestions.

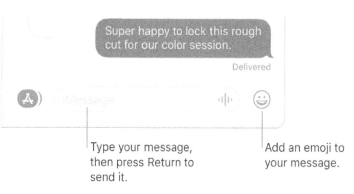

Type your message, then press Return to send it.

Add an emoji to your message.

Sending Your Message:

To send your message, either press the "Return" key on your keyboard or click the "Send" button in the top corner of a message.

Enhancing Your Messages:

The Messages app includes features like Tapbacks, the ability to attach photos, videos, stickers, audio messages, and use message effects to add flair to your conversations.

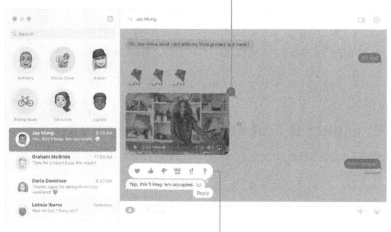

Conversation Management:

When you select tapback, it is sent straight away.

Conversations are organized in the sidebar of the Messages app, allowing you to easily switch between them and manage your messages.

Using Siri for Messages:

You can command Siri to send messages for you by stating, for example, "Message Mum that I'll be late."

When the message bubbles are green, it means they were sent as SMS text messages.

Important Information for Text and Multimedia Messages:

For sending SMS and MMS messages, ensure your iPhone runs iOS 8.1 or later, and both your Mac and iPhone are logged into iMessage with the

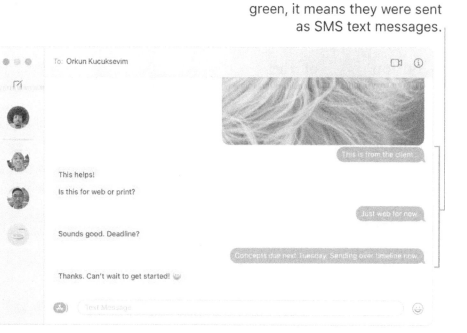

87

same Apple ID, which enables you to manage text and multimedia messages directly from your Mac.

FACETIME AND SHARE CONTENT IN MESSAGES ON YOUR MAC

Initiating FaceTime Video Calls via Messages:

1. Choose a conversation from your Messages.
2. Convey a message to an individual or group.
3. Click the "Video" button to start a FaceTime Video call with the selected contacts.

Click to hide the call window.

Picture-in-picture window

Move the pointer over FaceTime to see call options.

Managing the 'Shared with You' Feature in Messages:

To adjust 'Shared with You' for All Apps:

1. Open Messages 💬 on your Mac.
2. Navigate to Messages > Preferences, and click on "Shared with You."
3. To activate 'Shared with You' across all compatible apps, click "Turn On."
4. To deactivate, select "Turn Off."

Toggling 'Shared with You' by Conversation:

1. Within Messages, pick a conversation.
2. Click the "Info" button at the upper-right corner.
3. Check "Show in Shared with You" to have shared content show up in the appropriate app's 'Shared with You' area.
4. Uncheck to remove

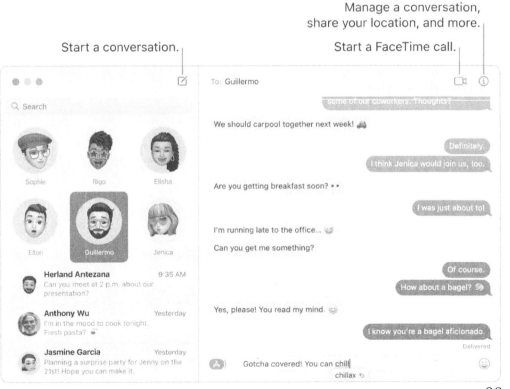

Start a conversation.

Manage a conversation, share your location, and more.

Start a FaceTime call.

content from this section.

Sharing Content with Contacts:
1. Choose the item you'd like to share, such as a webpage link.
2. Click the "Share" button ⬆ or select the Share option from the menu.
3. Pick "Messages."
4. In the "To" field, type your contact's details. Suggestions will appear as you type.
5. Optionally, add a message to accompany the shared item and then tap send to share.

Viewing Received Shared Content:
Shared items can be viewed in your Messages or within the respective apps that support 'Shared with You', like Apple TV, Safari, and others.
For instance, in Apple TV [tv], navigate to "Watch Now," then locate the 'Shared with You' section.

Continue the Conversation
In the corresponding apps, shared content includes a button with the name of the person who sent it. You can click this button to continue the conversation about the shared content. For example, in the News app , click the "From" label to send a reply in Messages.

Click to continue the conversation in Messages.

Pin Shared Content
If you find shared content particularly interesting, you can pin it in Messages, and it will be highlighted in Shared with You, Messages search, and the Info view of the conversation.

1. In the Messages app 🟢 on your Mac, select a conversation.
2. Control-click the shared content, then choose "Pin."

This way, you can easily keep track of the content shared with you and access it when it's convenient for you in various apps.

MUSIC

If you're someone who loves to explore a vast array of music, podcasts, and exclusive content, then setting up Apple Music on your Mac is the perfect way to unlock a world of audio entertainment. This guide will take you through the simple steps of subscribing and managing your Apple Music service, ensuring an enjoyable and hassle-free experience.

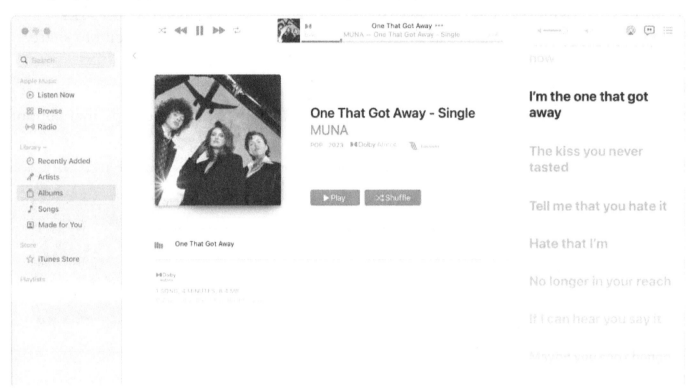

How to Subscribe to Apple Music on Your Mac

1. Launch the Music application 🎵 on your Mac.
2. From the top menu bar, navigate to "Account" and choose "Join Apple Music."
3. Complete the setup by following the prompts on your screen.
4. When required, log in with your Apple ID. If you do not have one, you will be given the option to create it during the process.

Once you become an Apple Music subscriber, you can enjoy the following benefits:

- Unlimited streaming of songs across a maximum of 10 different devices.
- Set your favorite artists to get updates and quick access to their tracks.
- The ability to download tunes for enjoying them offline.
- Full access to your music catalog on any device, anytime.
- Explore and play Apple Music's curated radio stations.
- SharePlay allows for a shared listening experience over FaceTime.

- Experience high-quality audio with lossless and Dolby Atmos selections.
- Create and share your musical preferences with an Apple Music profile.
- Open your Apple Music library to compatible third-party applications.
- Enjoy the lyrics of your favorite songs as they play.
- Autoplay feature keeps the music flowing by queuing up similar tracks.

To Manage Your Subscription:

1. Open the Music application 🎵 on your Mac and select "Account" > "Account Settings."
2. Sign in with your Apple ID if prompted.
3. Under the "Settings" section, click on "Manage" next to "Subscriptions."
4. Press "Edit" by Apple Music options to either cancel your subscription or modify your plan.

It's important to remember that the availability of Apple Music services can vary based on your geographical location.

By following these instructions, you'll be well on your way to enjoying all that Apple Music has to offer on your Mac. Please note that the availability of Apple Music, Apple Music Voice, and Apple One may vary by country or region.

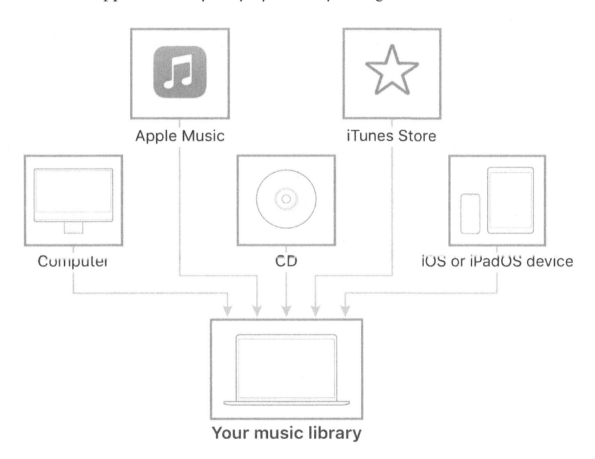

Dear Apple Pro!
I hope you are
enjoying exploring
the world of Apple
devices thus far!
Your feedback
means a lot to
me and it can be
a valuable gift to
fellow readers who
are considering this
guide. Writing a
review on Amazon
is a simple yet
incredibly helpful

way to pay it forward. Scan this QR code to take you straight there!

Your words have the power to inspire confidence in others, just as I've aimed to do with this book. Whether you found the content insightful, the instructions clear, or if you have any suggestions for improvement (I WILL incorporate it into following books), your review will be appreciated.

By sharing your thoughts, you not only assist other seniors in making an informed choice but also support the author (that's me!). If you made it this far, I am offering the digital beta copy of our next book for all customers in hopes for some feedback.

Email me at:
JasonBrownPublishing@gmail.com

Thank you for considering this request. Your words can make a big difference, and together, we can make the Apple world even more accessible and enjoyable for everyone, everywhere!

Thank you,
Jason Brown

NEWS

The News app 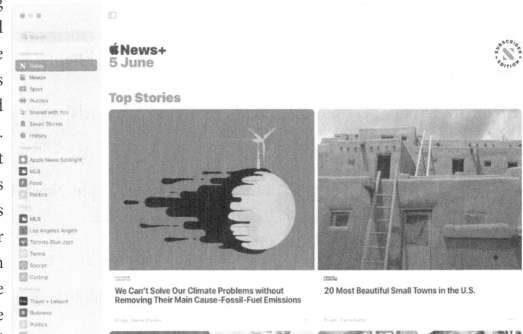 on your Mac is your personalized window into the world of journalism, offering a streamlined experience to browse and read the day's most important and interesting stories. With a sidebar that neatly categorizes content into Today's headlines, your Favorites, and even Apple News+, where a treasure trove of magazines and premium articles awaits, staying informed has never been easier. Whether you're looking for the latest in sports, interested in solving puzzles, or eager to read the top stories picked by Apple's editors, the News app delivers a rich and varied reading experience, all within a few clicks.

- Start by launching the News app on your Mac.
- You'll see a sidebar on the left side of the app window. This sidebar is the gateway to different sections of the app.
- If the sidebar is not visible, click the Sidebar button located in the toolbar to reveal it.

Understanding Sidebar Sections

Today: This section highlights top stories handpicked by Apple News editors and displays content from channels and topics you've shown interest in. In select locations, it even offers personalized local news and weather updates.

News+: Exclusive to Apple News+ subscribers, this tab gives you access to a library of magazines, leading newspapers, and premium online publications.

Puzzles Another perk for Apple News+ subscribers is the Puzzles section, where you can engage with daily crosswords.

Shared with You Find articles shared by friends through the Messages app all in one place for your convenience.

Sport: A dedicated space for sports enthusiasts to follow their preferred sports, leagues, and teams, complete with the latest scores and video highlights.

Favourites: This section lists your preferred channels and topics, which you can personalize at any time.

Suggested: Siri and your past interactions within Apple News tailor suggestions here, potentially including local news based on where you are.
Searching and Discovering New Content:

For topics or channels not immediately visible in the sidebar, you can use the search field at the top of the sidebar.
To uncover a wider range of channels, select "File" in the menu bar, then "Discover Channels."

NAVIGATING AND CUSTOMIZING YOUR READING EXPERIENCE IN THE NEWS APP

While Enjoying Articles

In the midst of reading, you have the option to watch accompanying videos, tailor your news feed by requesting more or fewer stories of that kind, share insightful pieces, or bookmark them to revisit later.
You can transition between stories with the simple press of the keyboard arrow keys.

Delve deeper into a publication by clicking the Share button in the toolbar, then selecting "Go to Channel."

To Follow Channels or Topics

1. Open the News app on your Mac.
2. For new channels or topics:
3. Choose "File" > "Discover Channels," select the channels you want to follow by

the icon should change to , and click "Done." Within the Today section, hit the "Add" button next to the channel or topic, or press the More (...) button and opt for "Follow Channel" or "Follow Topic."

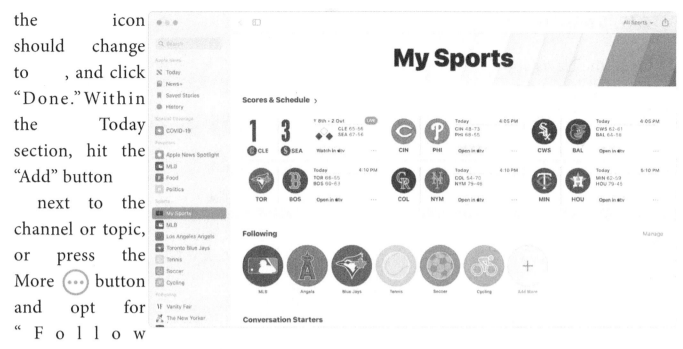

4. When viewing a specific topic or channel, use "File" > "Follow Topic" or "Follow Channel."

5. If you are enjoying a story, you can also choose "File" > "Follow Channel" or hit the Share button ⬆ and select "Follow Channel."

6. Utilize the search function to locate and follow channels or topics not immediately visible.

Unfollowing Made Simple

To unfollow, swipe over the channel or topic in the sidebar ▭ and select "Unfollow," or use the "File" menu for the same options.

When reading an article from a channel you wish to unfollow, click the Share button and choose "Unfollow Channel."

Organizing Favorites

Your Favorites hold the channels and topics you engage with most, and you can modify this list anytime.

To favorite, right-click the channel or topic under "Following" and select "Add to Favourites."

To unfollow, right-click an item under "Favourites" and choose "Remove from Favourites."

Rearrange your interests in the sidebar by dragging items under "Favourites" or "Following" to new positions.

Travel

VIEW SAVED STORIES

1. Open the News app 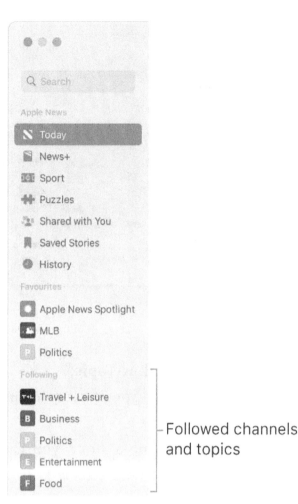 on your Mac.
2. In the sidebar (if not shown, click the Sidebar button ▢ in the toolbar), click "Saved Stories."
3. You will see a list of saved stories.
4. Click on a saved story to view it.
5. To return to the list of saved stories, click the "Back" ❮ button in the toolbar.

UNSAVE STORIES

1. To unsave a story, view the saved story in the News app on your Mac.
2. Click the "Save" button in the toolbar, or press Command-S.

NOTES

The Notes app on your Mac is a powerful and flexible tool designed to capture all your thoughts and ideas. Whether you're compiling a quick to-do list or assembling extensive research with checklists, images, and links, Notes has you covered. With collaboration features, you can work with others in real time, making it indispensable for team projects. Use mentions to

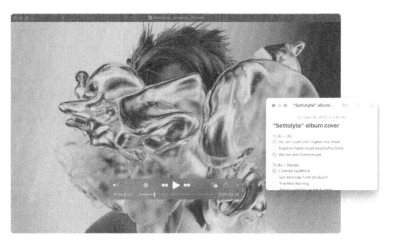

draw attention to important details, and organize your notes with customizable tags and Smart Folders for efficient retrieval. Thanks to iCloud Sync, your notes update across all your devices, ensuring you have the latest information wherever you go. And with Siri integration, creating new notes is as simple as speaking a command. The Notes app is the ultimate digital notebook for your personal and professional life.

Shared Note Editing:
Invite others to collaborate on shared notes and folders, enabling your team to collectively edit and update, which is ideal for group assignments and projects.

Direct Attention with Mentions:
Tag team members in a note to highlight important information or assign tasks, streamlining communication within your group.

Note Tags for Easy Sorting:
Utilize tags to categorize your notes. Whether it's by topic, project, or any custom label, tagging simplifies the retrieval and organization of your notes.

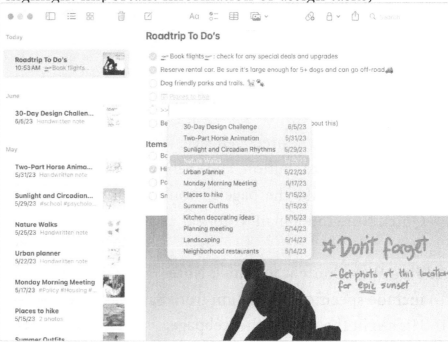

Automate with Smart Folders:

Smart Folders automatically sort your notes based on chosen criteria, such as checklists, attachments, or last modified dates, keeping your workspace tidy and efficient.

Access Anywhere with iCloud:

Thanks to iCloud sync, your notes update in real time across all your devices. Stay in sync with your thoughts and tasks no matter where you are or what device you're using.

Quick Creation with Siri:

For rapid note-taking, employ Siri's help. Just say, "Create a new note," and Siri will have it ready for you in an instant.

INITIATING A NEW QUICK NOTE

To ensure you start with a new Quick Note each time, navigate to "Notes" > "Settings" on your Mac and deselect the option for "Always resume to last Quick Note."

When you're in a different app and the urge to jot down a Quick Note strikes, here's how you can do it:

1. Using a Keyboard Shortcut: Simultaneously press and hold either the Fn or Globe key and then tap Q.
2. Employing Hot Corners: Glide your cursor to the screen's bottom-right edge (or your customized hot corner) and click on the note icon that pops up. Adjust or disable this feature in your Mac's system preferences.

Incorporating Safari Links into Quick Notes

While browsing in Safari **:**

1. Navigate to the desired webpage.
2. Click the "Share" button, and then pick "New Quick Note" or "Add to Quick Note."
3. This action links the page to your Quick Note, and revisiting the page will prompt a Quick Note thumbnail to appear as a handy reference.

Adding Web Content to Quick Notes

To include specific information from Safari into a Quick Note:

1. Highlight the text on the webpage.

2. Control-click the highlighted section and select "New Quick Note" or "Add to Quick Note."
3. The link and highlighted text will be saved, which will be highlighted again when you return to the page.

Managing Quick Notes

To close a Quick Note, simply click the red "Close" button ❌ at the top left of the note window. To reopen, use any of the methods previously mentioned for creating a Quick Note.

ORGANIZING NOTES AND ACCOUNTS

In the Notes app on your Mac, streamlining your note management is straightforward. You can enhance your organization by adding new accounts, pausing them, or removing them entirely. Here's how to navigate these options:

To Add an Account:

1. Launch the Notes app .
2. From the menu bar, select "Notes" > "Accounts."
3. Click "Add Account" and choose from account types like iCloud, Google, or Yahoo.
4. Complete the sign-in process with your credentials, and make sure to check the "Notes" option for the account.
5. Hit "Done" to finalize adding the account.

Each account appears separately in the Notes app, and to ensure your notes are up-to-date on all devices, add the same accounts to your other Apple devices like the iPhone or iPad.

To Pause an Account Temporarily:

In the Notes app , head to "Notes" in the menu bar.

Click "Accounts" and select the account you wish to disable.

Deselect "Notes" to make the notes from this account temporarily inaccessible.

Your notes won't be visible while "Notes" is turned off, but you can re-enable it anytime to regain access.

To Remove an Account:

1. Open the Notes app .

2. Go to "Notes" > "Accounts" in the menu.

3. Select the account you intend to delete.

4. Choose "Delete Account."

Removing an account will delete its notes from your Mac, but they'll remain in the cloud service associated with that account and on any other devices where the account is active.

ENHANCING NOTES WITH MULTIMEDIA AND FILES

With the Notes app on your Mac, enriching your notes with various attachments is a straightforward process. Here's how you can incorporate more than just text into your notes:

Adding Attachments to Notes:

Open the Notes app and select an existing note or create a new one. (Remember, locked notes need to be unlocked first.)

To attach a file, simply drag it from the Desktop or Finder into your note.

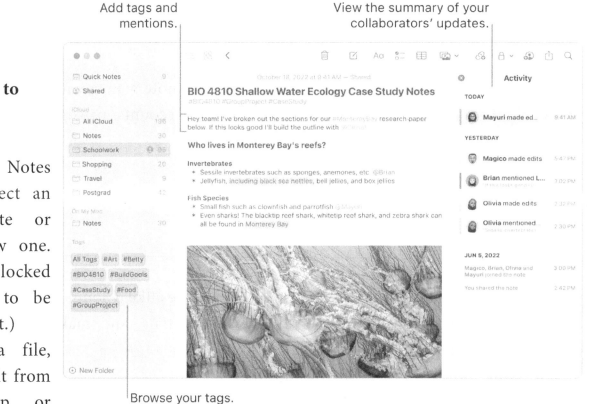

Add tags and mentions.

View the summary of your collaborators' updates.

Browse your tags.

Alternatively, go to "Edit" > "Attach File," select the desired file, and click "Attach."

For photos, drag them from your Photos library directly into the note, or use the 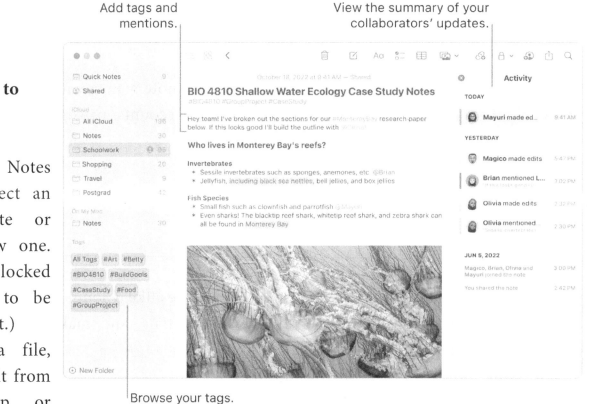 button in the Notes toolbar to navigate to "Photos" and drag an image in.

Capturing Content with iPhone or iPad:

To insert a photo or scan, click where you want it in the note, then "File" > "Insert from iPhone or iPad." Choose either "Take Photo" or "Scan Documents."

To add a sketch, click in your note, then "File" > "Insert from iPhone or iPad" > "Add Sketch." Use your finger or Apple Pencil to create the sketch.

Add a checklist, table, photo, scan, or sketch.

Collaborate or send a copy.

Change text format.

Add link

Lock note.

Adjusting Attachment Sizes:

Change the size of all images, scanned documents, or PDFs by selecting "View" > "Attachment View," then choose your preferred size for all attachments.

For individual adjustments, Control-click the attachment, select "View As," and pick a size. (Note that you cannot resize drawings.)

Adding Content from Other Apps:

In apps like Maps or Safari, use the "Share" button , select "Notes," and save to either a new or existing note.

You can share selected text or images by Control-clicking the selection, choosing "Share," then "Notes," and saving it.

By following these steps, your notes can become more dynamic, visual, and informative, turning them into comprehensive documents that go beyond simple text.

A Shared icon shows the note is shared with one or more people.

Summer Outfits
Yesterday 2 photos

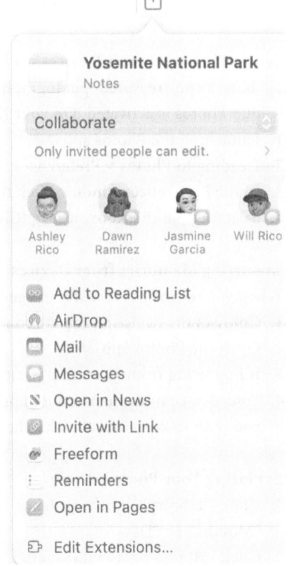

PHOTOS

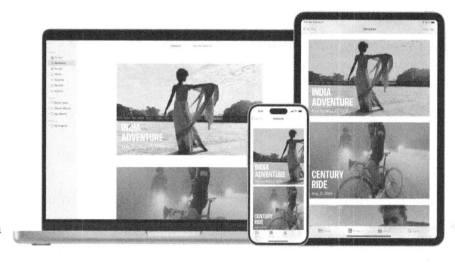

The Photos app on a Mac is an all-in-one digital asset management program that not only stores and organizes your pictures and videos but also provides powerful editing tools for enhancing your media. With iCloud integration, it ensures your memories are kept in sync across all your devices. Ideal for everyday photo viewing, meticulous organization, or creative editing, the Photos app is essential for anyone looking to preserve, share, and work with their photographic memories. Whether you're compiling albums for a family reunion, touching up snapshots for social media, or simply enjoying a stroll down memory lane, Photos supports these experiences with ease and efficiency.

Syncing Photos Across Devices via iCloud

To have your treasured photographs synchronized across all your devices, make sure iCloud Photos is activated. On your Mac, you can do this by:

1. Launching the Photos app .
2. Heading to Photos > Preferences.
3. In the Preferences window, click the iCloud tab.
4. Selecting the checkbox next to iCloud Photos.

Importing Memories from Devices

When you're ready to transfer images from an iPhone, iPad, or camera to your Mac:

1. Connect the device or camera to your Mac, ensuring it's switched on.
2. Open the Photos app .
3. If importing from a camera, put it in the mode that allows photo transfers.
4. Your device or camera should appear in the sidebar. Click on it, choose the snapshots you wish to keep, and then hit the "Import Selected" button.

Exploring Your Photo Library

1. Click "Library" in the sidebar to explore by time frame, choosing from "Years," "Months," or "Days."
2. Click "All Photos" to view every image in your collection.

3. Use the "People" or "Places" options in faces or locations.

Editing for Perfection

If a photo needs trimming or straightening:

1. Double-click on the image.
2. Hit "Edit" on the toolbar.
3. Choose "Crop."
4. Adjust the frame to fit the part of the image you want to focus on, and use the "Straighten" dial to align it just right.

Enhancing Your Photos

To give your photos a little extra flair:

1. Double-click the photo you want to improve.
2. Click "Edit" in the toolbar.
3. Use "Light" or "Colour" to fine-tune your photo.
4. Adjust the sliders until you're satisfied or select "Auto" for automatic enhancements.

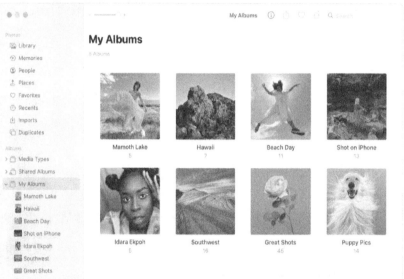

Managing Photo Storage Efficiently

For keeping your Mac's storage from filling up, while using iCloud Photos:

1. Open the Photos app 🌸.
2. Choose Photos from the menu bar.
3. Navigate to Preferences and select the iCloud tab. Here you can opt to store originals

or keep only space-efficient versions on your Mac, while the full-resolution originals remain in iCloud.

Restoring Full-Size Photos and Managing Storage

To switch from storing optimized photos to keeping the full-size originals on your Mac, you can adjust the settings in the Photos app with a few easy steps:

1. Open the Photos app ✻ on your Mac.
2. In the menu bar at the top of the screen, click on "Photos" and then choose "Preferences."
3. Click the "iCloud" tab within the Preferences window.
4. Look for the "Optimise Mac Storage" option and deselect it.
5. With this change, the Photos app will start downloading the original, high-resolution photos to your Mac. This may take some time, especially if you have a large library or slow internet connection.

Deleting Photos and Videos

1. Open the Photos app ✻.
2. Select the items you wish to delete.
3. Press the Delete key to move them to the "Recently Deleted" album, where they will stay for 30 days before permanent deletion.

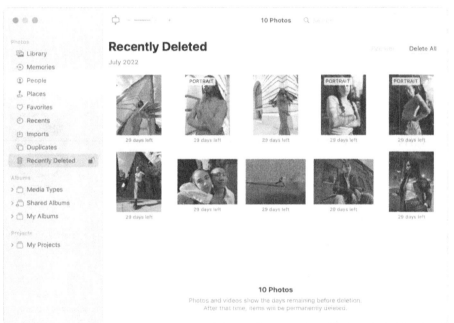

Restoring Recently Deleted Items

If you've accidentally deleted something:

1. Open the "Recently Deleted" album from the sidebar in the Photos app ✻.
2. Select the items you want to recover.
3. Click "Recover" to restore them back to your library.
4. Remember, if you're using iCloud Photos, you can retrieve items from any device within 30 days. Without iCloud Photos, they're only deleted from your Mac.

Recovering from Time Machine

If you have Time Machine set up, you might be able to restore items that have been permanently deleted.

Using iCloud Photos

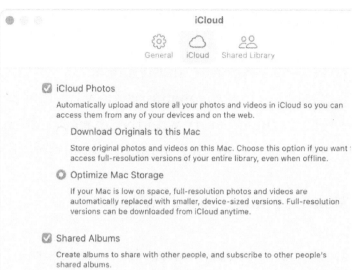

To enable iCloud Photos on your Mac for cross-device photo access:

1. Make sure you're signed in with your Apple ID on your Mac.
2. Open the Photos app 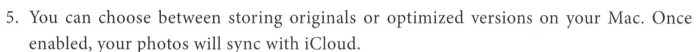 .
3. Click "Photos" in the top menu, then "Preferences."
4. In the iCloud tab, check the "iCloud Photos" box.
5. You can choose between storing originals or optimized versions on your Mac. Once enabled, your photos will sync with iCloud.

To disable iCloud Photos

1. Open the Photos app preferences.
2. Under the iCloud tab, uncheck "iCloud Photos."
3. Decide whether to download photos or remove incomplete downloads.
4. Disabling iCloud Photos on your Mac leaves the photos in iCloud and accessible to other devices with iCloud Photos turned on.

ENJOYING AND CRAFTING MEMORIES IN THE PHOTOS APP

Playing a Memory

1. Launch the Photos app on your Mac and select "Memories" from the sidebar.
2. Browse and choose a memory that catches your eye.
3. Double-click a memory to play it.
4. Control playback by clicking the Play button or pressing the Spacebar. Navigate through photos using arrow keys or swipes.
5. For a grid view of the memory's photos, click the "Grid View" button.
6. To exit, click the left arrow in the toolbar.

Creating Your Own Memory from an Album

1. In the sidebar, select an album you love.
2. Click "Play Memory Video" in the toolbar to generate a memory.

3. To keep it in your Memories, hit the "Favourite" button. If you reconsider, click the button again to unfavorite it.

Sharing a Memory

1. Go to "Memories" in the sidebar.
2. Double-click the memory you wish to share.
3. Pause the memory with the Spacebar, then click the "Share" button ⬆.
4. Choose the sharing method you prefer, such as Messages, Mail, or AirDrop.

Sharing Photos from a Memory

1. Navigate to "Memories" in the sidebar.
2. Open the memory with the photos you want to share.
3. Stop the memory with the Spacebar, then select "Grid View."
4. Pick the photos and hit the "Share" button   .
5. Select how you'd like to share, whether it's via Messages, Mail, or using AirDrop.

Adding a Memory as a Favorite

1. In "Memories," find a memory to favorite.
2. Click the "Favourite" button on the memory or while it's playing.
3. To revisit your favorites, select "Favourite Memories" in the toolbar.

These features in the Photos app allow you to relive and share your cherished moments with ease, turning your photos into stories and experiences to be enjoyed over and over again.

DISABLING ICLOUD PHOTOS ACROSS APPLE DEVICES

1. On your Mac, begin by clicking the Apple menu and selecting "System Preferences."
2. Click on your name at the top of the sidebar; if you're not signed in, do so with your Apple ID.
3. Choose "iCloud" and then "Manage."
4. Select "Photos" and opt for "Turn Off and Delete."

Caution: Disabling iCloud Photos will remove all your photos and videos from iCloud after 30 days. If you have a change of heart, use the "Undo Delete" option within this period to recover your media.

Playing a Memory

1. Open the Photos app on your Mac and select "Memories" from the sidebar.
2. Browse and double-click a memory to play it.
3. Control playback with the Play button or Spacebar, and navigate through photos with arrow keys or swipes.
4. Use the "Grid View" button to see all the photos in the memory, and the left arrow to exit.

Automatically create a personalized video of special moments.

View your photos by Years, Months, Days, or All Photos.

Creating a Memory from an Album

1. Choose an album from the sidebar.
2. Click "Play Memory Video" in the toolbar.
3. To save it to Memories, click the "Favourite" button; click again to unfavourite.

Sharing a Memory

1. Go to "Memories" in the sidebar.
2. Double-click a memory to select it.
3. Stop it with the Spacebar, then click the "Share" button.
4. Decide on the sharing method: Messages, Mail, or AirDrop.

Sharing Photos from a Memory

1. From "Memories," open the desired memory.
2. Stop the playback, then click "Grid View."
3. Select photos and click "Share" in the toolbar.
4. Choose how to share: Messages, Mail, or AirDrop.

Favoriting a Memory

1. In "Memories," scroll to find a memory to favourite.
2. Click the "Favourite" button on the memory.
3. Access your favourite memories under "Favourite Memories" in the toolbar.
4. By following these steps, you can effectively manage your iCloud Photos and fully enjoy the Memories feature in the Photos app on your Mac.

PODCASTS

The Podcasts app 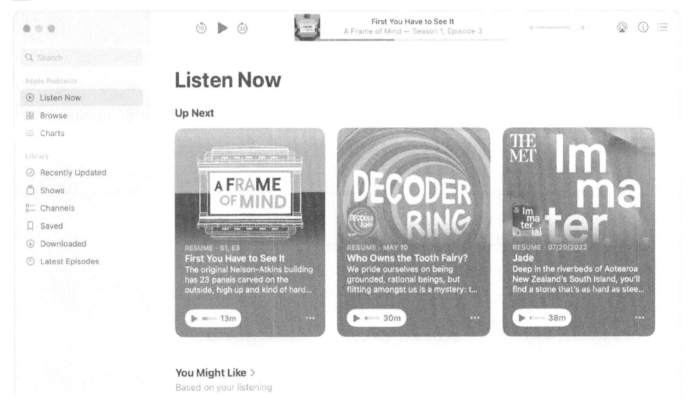 on Mac is an immersive audio platform that offers a vast array of shows and episodes right at your fingertips. Whether you're looking to stay updated with your favorite series, explore new and trending topics, or simply keep your digital library organized, Apple Podcasts stands ready to cater to your listening desires. Integrated with Siri for hands-free control, featuring seamless iCloud syncing for cross-device listening, and offering personalized recommendations, this app is a robust tool for podcast enthusiasts. The intuitive interface, coupled with powerful search capabilities and easy library management, ensures a user-friendly experience. With the added convenience of Quick Note for jotting down thoughts and AirPlay for superior listening, the Podcasts app is a comprehensive solution for audio discovery and enjoyment on your Mac.

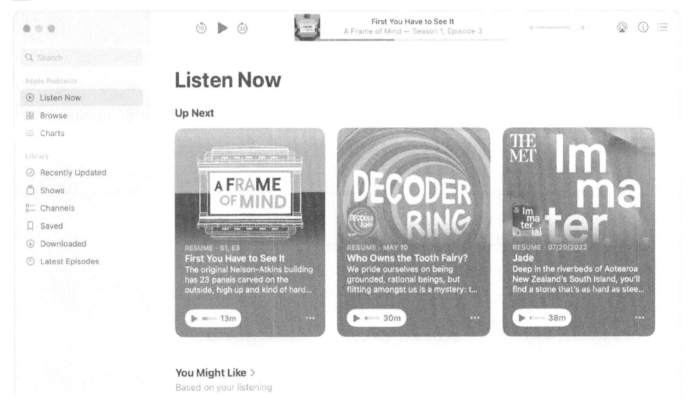

Apple Podcasts on Mac

Apple Podcasts app on your Mac for podcast enthusiasts and newcomers alike, providing a rich library of shows across all genres. Here's a beginner-friendly guide to help you tap into the vast world of stories, educational content, discussions, and more:

Listen Now for Personalized Picks:

Dive into the 'Listen Now' tab to explore podcasts you're already following or discover new ones curated to your taste. With Siri's help, you can easily navigate your podcasts and resume episodes right where you left off.

Discovering New Favorites:

Venture through the 'Listen Now' section to stumble upon fresh podcasts that pique your interest. Subscribe to keep up with the latest episodes or save them for later. Don't forget to check the 'Top Charts' for trending content.

Shared with You:

Episodes shared by friends in Messages find their home in 'Shared with You,' making sure you're in the loop with the podcasts your circle loves.

Curate Your Library:

Spot an episode you're interested in? Click 'Add' ┼ to save it to your library. Hit 'Subscribe' to a podcast to automatically update your feed with new episodes, and download them using the download button ⬇ to listen online.for offline indulgence.

Search Smarter:

Find podcasts featuring your favorite hosts or special guests with a quick search, which neatly presents relevant episodes and mentions.

Never Miss an Episode:

Use the 'Follow' feature to keep your most-loved shows at the forefront of your library, ensuring you're always caught up with the latest releases.

Remember with Quick Note:

When a podcast sparks an idea or you want to jot down a thought for later, Quick Note is there to capture it. Easily access these notes later in the Notes app.

Enhance Your Listening Experience with AirPlay:

Amplify your listening experience by streaming podcasts through your favorite external speakers via AirPlay. Just click the Control Center icon and select your speaker to start the show.

Apple Podcasts on your Mac is more than just an app—it's a gateway to learning, entertainment, and connection with voices from around the globe, all at your fingertips.

PREVIEW

Explore the multifaceted Preview app on your Mac, a comprehensive tool for handling PDFs and images with an array of editing features. With Preview, you can effortlessly interact with documents, from straightforward viewing and editing to filling out and digitally signing forms.

Simple Edits on PDFs and Images:
 Open, view, and perform basic edits on PDFs and images directly within Preview.

Interactive Form Filling:
Easily fill out PDF forms by typing in the text fields provided.

Enhanced PDF Security:
Safeguard your PDFs by setting up passwords to restrict access to the document's contents.

PDF Page Management: Add, delete, or reorder pages to tailor your PDF documents to your exact needs.

PDF Page Transfers:
Effortlessly transfer pages between PDFs with Preview's copy-and-paste functionality—perfect for merging information from different sources.

On-the-Spot Translation:
Quickly translate selected PDF text with a simple right-click and choose "Translate," making it possible to understand content in multiple languages, even offline.

Flexible Image Conversion:
Open and convert images among various formats, such as JPEG, PDF, PNG, TIFF, streamlining your workflow in handling image files.

Preview stands as your go-to app for document and image management, offering user-friendly features that cater to both personal and professional demands on your Mac.

REMINDERS

Keeping track of tasks and to-dos can be challenging, but the Reminders app on your Mac can help you stay organized. To make the most of the app, here are some tips and features you can use:

Tags: You can add tags to your reminders to help organize them. By clicking on one or more tags in the sidebar, you can quickly filter reminders based on those tags.

Custom Smart Lists: Smart Lists automatically sort your upcoming reminders based on criteria like dates, times, tags, locations, flags, or priority. To create your own Custom Smart Lists, simply add filters to suit your specific needs.

Save Lists as Templates: If you have a list that you want to reuse in the future, you can save it as a template. Simply select the list in the sidebar, then choose "File > Save as Template."

Today and Scheduled Lists: The Today and Scheduled lists in the sidebar group reminders based on their due dates and times. This helps you keep track of what's coming up and ensures you don't miss any important tasks.

Smart Suggestions: Reminders can automatically suggest dates, times, and locations for a reminder based on your past reminders. This feature can save you time when creating new reminders.

Collaboration: You can collaborate with others on a list by sending invitations through Messages or Mail, or by sharing a link. Click the Share button , then choose how to share the list. Once others are invited, you can track activity and manage collaboration using the Collaborate button .

Assign Responsibility: When sharing a list, you can assign reminders to specific people, ensuring that they receive notifications. This is useful for dividing tasks and clarifying responsibilities.

Subtasks and Groups: You can create subtasks by pressing Command-] or dragging one reminder on top of another. Subtasks are indented under their parent reminders. You can also organize your lists by creating groups. To create a group, choose "File > New Group."
111

Completed Smart List: The Completed Smart List in the sidebar allows you to review all your finished reminders, including their completion dates.

Reminder Suggestions in Mail: When using Mail, Siri can recognize potential reminders and make suggestions for creating them. This feature can be especially helpful during email correspondence.

Adding Reminders Quickly: You can add reminders quickly using natural language. For instance, you can type "Take Amy to soccer every Wednesday at 5 PM" to create a repeating reminder for that specific day and time.

By using these features and tips, you can make the most of the Reminders app on your Mac and stay organized with your tasks and to-dos.

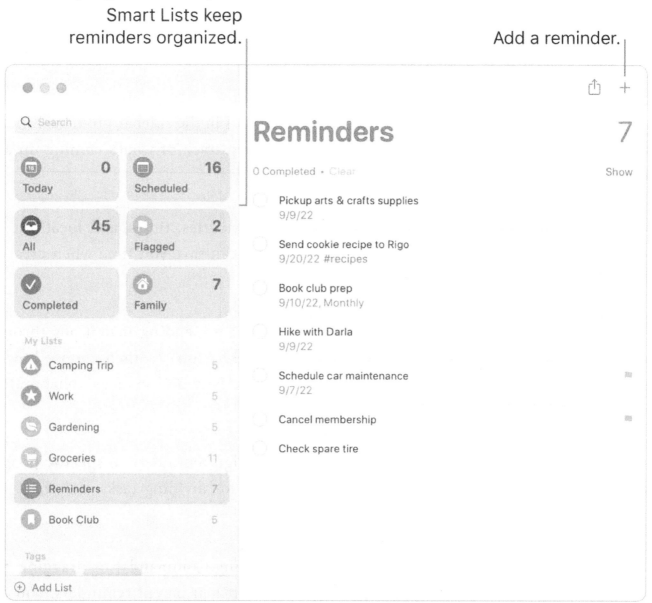

SAFARI

Safari is not just a web browser; it's your personal passageway to the endless expanse of the internet, crafted specifically for your Mac. Whether you're diving into research, shopping online, or streaming your favorite series, Safari delivers a fast, secure, and energy-efficient browsing experience. With its user-friendly Smart Search field, you're one click away from finding everything from the nearest gelato spot to scholarly articles on quantum physics. Choose Safari for those moments when you want a browsing experience that's as smart and sophisticated as your Mac itself.

Effortless Web Search:

Just type your query into the Smart Search field—be it "best coffee shops" or "local weather"—and select from the predictive search suggestions.

Type what you're looking for.

Direct Website Access:

Enter a site's name or URL into the same field to navigate directly to your online destination.

Personalize Your Homepage:

Make your favorite site the first thing you see by setting it as your homepage under Safari > Preferences > General.

Bookmark with Ease:

Keep track of your go-to sites by bookmarking them. Hit the Share button ⬆️, then "Add Bookmark," and find them anytime in the Bookmarks list from the Sidebar ▢.

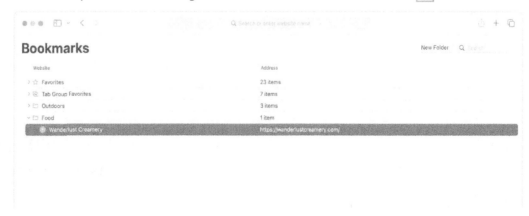

Transform any website into a Mac app with Safari's unique feature!

This action pins the website to your Dock and Launchpad, creating a web app experience. If you're already logged into the site, your credentials should carry over seamlessly.

Enjoy the benefits of a web app, including a streamlined toolbar and real-time notifications, turning your most-visited sites into readily accessible apps on your Mac. To do this:

1. Open Safari on your Mac.
2. Navigate to your desired website.
3. Look for the Share button in the Safari toolbar—it's the icon resembling a square with an upward arrow.
4. In the dropdown Share menu, choose "Add to Dock."
5. Confirm by clicking "Add."

Creating Browsing Profiles in Safari

Keep your browsing experiences compartmentalized with profiles in Safari:

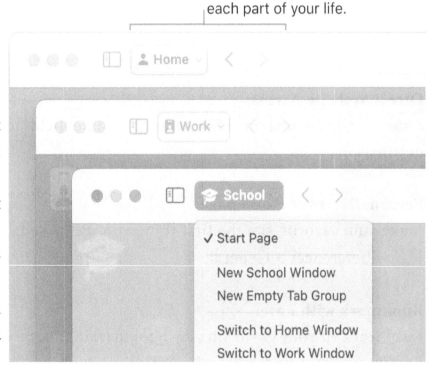

Create a profile for each part of your life.

1. Launch Safari.
2. Go to the top menu, select "Safari" > "Settings," and then navigate to "Profiles."
3. For first-timers, select "Start Using Profiles."
4. Click the "Add" button to initiate a new profile.
5. Name your profile, pick an icon and color, and associate a bookmarks folder with it.
6. Finish by clicking "Create Profile."

You can also manage browser extensions for each profile individually. Remember, passwords saved in iCloud Keychain are accessible across all profiles.

Besides any new profiles, there's always a "Personal (Default)" profile which you can customize too. Profiles are perfect for maintaining distinct browsing environments for various facets of your digital life.

SECURING PRIVATE BROWSING IN SAFARI ON MAC

To add a layer of security to your private browsing sessions in Safari with a password or Touch ID:

Private Browsing Is Locked

Touch ID or enter the password for the user "Danny Rico" to view locked tabs.

Enter password

1. Launch Safari 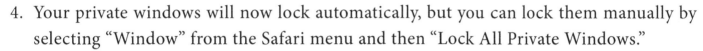 and head to "Settings" from the Safari menu.
2. Navigate to "Privacy."
3. Within Privacy, choose "Require password to view locked tabs" or "Require Touch ID to view locked tabs" depending on your device capabilities.
4. Your private windows will now lock automatically, but you can lock them manually by selecting "Window" from the Safari menu and then "Lock All Private Windows."

These private windows will also lock automatically when you engage screen lock, start a screensaver, switch off the display, leave the windows minimized for a while, or if they're open in the background without activity for some time.

To **disable** this feature, simply deselect the password or Touch ID option in the Privacy settings.

Managing Pop-ups or extra windows/ads that pop up in Safari

Click to show the blocked pop-up windows.

To control pop-ups across all websites:

Show blocked pop-up window

1. Open Safari and go to "Settings."
2. Block and Notify: Pop-ups for all websites won't appear, but you'll be notified when a pop-up is blocked, and you can choose to show it by clicking the "Show" button in the Smart Search field.

Adjust pop-up settings under "When visiting other websites" by choosing to allow, block and notify, or block pop-ups.

Remember, blocking pop-ups might impact your browsing experience by hiding content you might want to see. Persistent pop-ups, despite being blocked, may indicate the presence of unwanted software.

Clearing Cookies in Safari

To clear cookies:

1. Open Safari  and select "Preferences" from the menu.
2. Click the "Privacy" tab.
3. Hit "Manage Website Data."
4. You can then choose to remove data from specific sites or remove all website data.

Be aware that clearing cookies might log you out of sites and change how they function. This action can also affect cookies in other applications linked to Safari.

PRIVATE BROWSING IN SAFARI ON YOUR MAC

Here's what happens in Private Browsing:
Your browsing is compartmentalized, keeping different tabs separate to prevent cross-site tracking.

The webpages you visit, along with AutoFill data, won't be recorded.

Open webpages aren't saved to iCloud, thus not syncing across your Apple devices.

The Smart Search field won't display your recent searches.

Downloaded items won't show up in Safari's downloads list (although they will be on your computer).

No changes are stored for cookies and website data.

To explore the web on your Mac without leaving a digital footprint, you can easily initiate a private browsing session in Safari:

1. Launch Safari 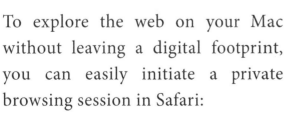.

2. From the Safari menu, select "File" and then "New Private Window."

3. A window with a dark Smart Search field will appear, signaling that you're in private browsing mode.

To set Safari to always open in Private Browsing mode:

1. Go to "Safari" > "Settings" > "General" and set "Safari opens with" to "A new private window."

When you're ready to return to regular browsing:

Simply close the private window, or open a new window in the standard browsing mode. Keep in mind, private browsing ensures your session information isn't kept, giving you a cleaner and more secure online experience.

STOCKS

Equipped with the necessary features and functionalities, the Stocks app 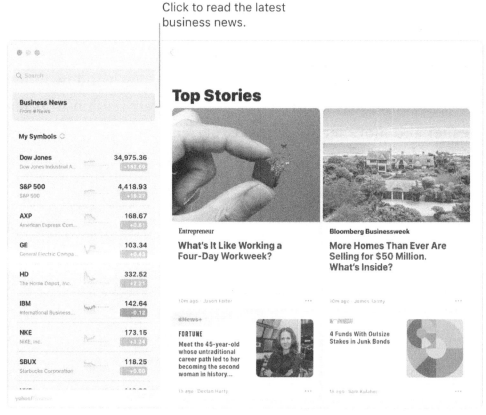 on your Mac is an essential tool for keeping an eye on financial markets and your investments. Below are the key attributes and how to utilize them to your advantage:

Create and Personalize Watchlists

1. Initiate a new watchlist by clicking on "My Symbols" and select "New Watchlist."
2. To add stocks to your watchlist, simply enter a company name or stock symbol in the search field and double-click on the stock symbol in the search results to view detailed stock information.
3. To add a stock to a watchlist, click the "Add" button in the top-right corner, and choose the watchlist you want to add it to.

Click to read the latest business news.

4. To remove a stock from a watchlist, Control-click on the stock symbol and select "Manage Symbol." Then, deselect the checkbox next to the watchlist you want to remove it from.
- Control-clicking a stock in your watchlist will allow you to open it in a new tab or window.

Monitor Market Fluctuations

- In your watchlist, you can view real-time market data and switch between price change, percentage change, and market capitalization by clicking on the green or red button below each price.
- Color-coded sparklines provide a visual representation of the stock's performance throughout the day.

Read Articles

1. Click on a stock in your watchlist to access an interactive chart and additional details about that stock.
2. You can also read the latest news related to the company.
3. To access curated business articles from Apple News, click "Business News" at the top of your watchlist.

Get a Deeper View

The Stocks app allows you to explore historical data. You can switch between different timeframes (e.g., last week, last month, or last year) by clicking the buttons above the chart.

Sync Watchlists Across Devices

By signing in with the same Apple ID on multiple devices, you can ensure that your watchlist remains consistent across all of them, providing you access to the same information on all your Apple devices.

Please note that Apple News stories and Top Stories are available in the U.S., Canada, the UK, and Australia, while news stories in other countries and regions are provided by Yahoo.

Click to cycle between price change, percentage change, and market capitalization.

APPLE TV

The Apple TV app on your Mac is the hub for all your TV and streaming content. It offers a range of features that make it easy for you to access your favorite content.

Here's what you can do with the Apple TV app:

1. **Apple TV+:** Subscribe to and watch Apple TV+, Apple's streaming service featuring original TV shows and movies created by some of the most creative people in the entertainment industry. Note that the availability of Apple TV+ varies by country and region.

2. **MLS Season Pass:** If you're a fan of Major League Soccer (MLS), you can subscribe to MLS Season Pass in the Apple TV app. This provides access to all MLS regular season and playoff matches and hundreds of MLS NEXT Pro and MLS NEXT games. Note that the availability of MLS Season Pass may differ depending on your location.

3. **Apple TV Channels:** You can subscribe to various Apple TV channels, such as Paramount+ and STARZ, to access additional content. The availability of Apple TV channels may differ by country and region.

4. **Personalized Recommendations:** The app offers content recommendations based on your viewing history and preferences, making it easier to discover new shows and movies you might enjoy.

5. **Content Sharing:** You can watch movies and shows shared with you from the Messages app.

6. **Watch Together with SharePlay:** The Apple TV app integrates with SharePlay and the FaceTime app, allowing you to watch content with friends and family, even if you're not in the same location.

7. **Access the Store:** You can access the Apple TV Store to purchase, rent, or subscribe to

the world's best movies and TV shows, including Apple TV channels that you haven't subscribed to yet.

8. **Manage Your Collection:** The app provides access to your entire movie and TV show collection, making it easy to organize and access your media.

Keep in mind that the availability of some features, such as Apple TV+ and MLS Season Pass, may vary by country or region. This means that the content and subscriptions available to you in the Apple TV app could differ based on your location.

Sign in to start watching now

To buy, rent, or subscribe to content on Apple TV app using your Mac, you need to sign in with your Apple ID. Here's how you can sign in or create a new Apple ID if you don't have one yet:

Creating a New Apple ID

1. Open the Apple TV app  on your Mac.
2. Click on "Account" in the menu bar at the top of the screen.
3. Choose "Sign In."
4. Click on "Create New Apple ID."
5. Follow the on-screen instructions to set up a new Apple ID.

Please note that PayPal is available as a payment method in some regions. However, it may not be accepted in all countries.

Signing In or Out of the Apple TV app

Once you have an Apple ID, you can use it to sign in or out of the Apple TV app. Here's how:

1. In the Apple TV app  on your Mac, click on "Account" in the menu bar.
2. Select either "Sign In" or "Sign Out," depending on your current status.
3. If you can't remember your Apple ID or password, click on "Forgot Apple ID or Password?" and follow the instructions to recover your credentials.

We recommend signing out of the app if you share your computer with others to prevent unauthorized purchases using your account.

By signing in, you can easily access your account information, purchase history, and enjoy a seamless experience when renting or buying movies and TV shows through the Apple TV app 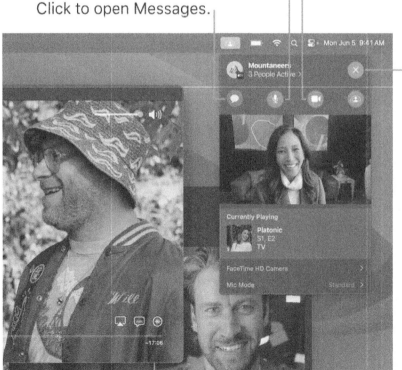tv

Watch together

Watching movies or TV shows with your friends or family can be a fun activity, especially when you are not together physically. With SharePlay in the Apple TV app, you can enjoy synchronized viewing while on a FaceTime call.

Watch together with SharePlay

1. Open the FaceTime app on your Mac and start or answer a call.
2. Open the Apple TV app tv on your Mac or another caller's device and start watching a movie or show.
3. If prompted, click "View" to open the TV app on your Mac and then click "Join."

The video will start playing in sync on all devices participating in the FaceTime call. Each person can control the playback using their respective devices while the FaceTime app window remains open.

To modify the SharePlay settings, you can click the SharePlay button in the macOS menu bar.

Leaving the call or shared viewing session

Anyone can leave the FaceTime call while continuing the shared viewing session or leave both. Here is how you can do it:

1. While using SharePlay in the Apple TV app tv

Click to turn off your camera.

Click to mute your microphone.

Click to open Messages.

Click to leave the call

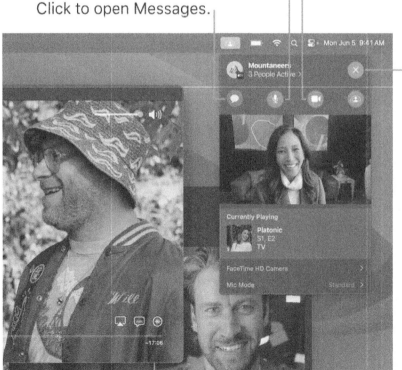

on your Mac, click the SharePlay button in the macOS menu bar.

2. Click the "Leave Call" button ⊗.
3. Choose to either "Continue" or "Leave SharePlay."

If you initiated the shared session and choose "Leave SharePlay," the shared session will end for everyone.

Start a text conversation

During a SharePlay watch session in the Apple TV app tv on your Mac, you can initiate a text conversation in Messages with all the participants:

1. Click the SharePlay button in the macOS menu bar.
2. Click the "Messages" button ○.
3. The Messages app will open, allowing you to enter your messages in the text field.
4.

Add video effects

While watching with SharePlay, you can add video effects and animated reactions to your live video in the FaceTime app window (requires macOS 12 or later and Apple silicon):

1. Click the SharePlay button in the macOS menu bar.
2. Click the disclosure arrow to the right of "FaceTime HD Camera."
3. Choose video effects such as Portrait, Studio Light, or Reactions (animated effects created using hand gestures).
4.

Adjust microphone sensitivity

You can adjust the sensitivity of your microphone to isolate your voice or capture surrounding sounds (requires macOS 12 or later and Apple silicon):

1. Click the SharePlay button in the macOS menu bar.
2. Click the disclosure triangle to the right of "Mic Mode."
3. Select a microphone option: Standard, Voice Isolation, or Wide Spectrum.

Use AirPlay

If you want to share what you're watching during SharePlay with an Apple TV on the same network:

1. While using SharePlay in the Apple TV app tv on your Mac, move your pointer over the viewer window to show playback controls.
2. Click the AirPlay button and choose the Apple TV you want to use for watching.
123

VOICE MEMOS

Your personal dictaphone!

Voice Memos app  on the Mac is a straightforward and efficient app that allows you to quickly record personal notes, meetings, lectures, and musical ideas. With a user-friendly interface, it enables one-click recording, easy organizational features like folders and favorites, and seamless iCloud integration to access memos across all Apple devices.

Enhanced playback options like speed control and skip silence, along with audio enhancement capabilities, make Voice Memos a versatile app for anyone looking to capture and manage audio with ease.

How to Record

Open the voice memos app on your MacBook

1. To start a new recording, press the red Record button .
2. When you're finished, click the Done button to stop recording.

Renaming Your Recording:

To change the recording's name, click on the name that appears and type in something new that describes your recording.

Listening to Your Recording:

To hear your recording, click the Play button .

Using Your Recordings on Different Devices:

If you sign in with your Apple ID, you can listen to your voice memos on any of your devices, like your iPad or iPhone.

Keeping Recordings Organized:

Click the Sidebar button (it looks like a little square) to show the sidebar, then click the New Folder button at the bottom to make a folder.

Type in a name for your folder and click Save.

To move a recording into this new folder, hold down the Option key on your keyboard and drag the recording into the folder.

Saving Important Recordings

Click on a recording to select it, then click the Favorite button to mark it as important. To see all your important recordings, click the Sidebar button .

Skipping Quiet Parts in Recordings

To skip parts where there's no talking, click the Playback Settings button (it looks like a little gear) and choose "Skip Silence."

Changing How Fast/Slow the Recording Plays

In the Playback Settings, you can make the recording play faster or slower by moving the speed slider left or right.

Making Your Recording Sound Clearer:

To reduce background noise, click "Enhance Recording" in the Playback Settings.

These steps will help you record, organize, and listen to all your voice memos easily on your MacBook.

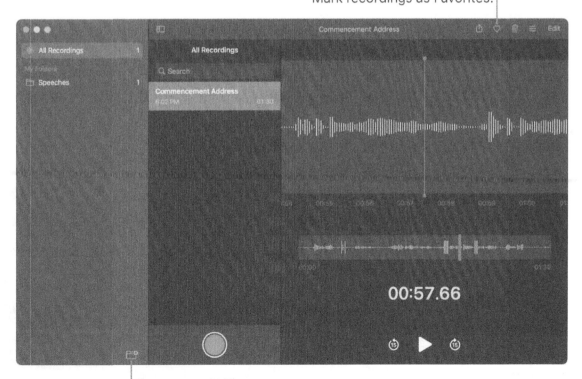

Mark recordings as Favorites.

Create new folders to organize your recordings.

Dear Apple Pro!
I hope you have enjoyed exploring the world of Apple devices. Your feedback means a lot to me and it can be a valuable gift to fellow readers who are considering this guide. Writing a review on Amazon is a simple yet incredibly helpful

way to pay it forward(Do not worry, its free!). Scan this QR code to take you straight there!

Your words have the power to inspire confidence in others, just as I've aimed to do with this book. Whether you found the content insightful, the instructions clear, or if you have any suggestions for improvement (I WILL incorporate it into following books), your review will be appreciated.

By sharing your thoughts, you not only assist other seniors in making an informed choice but also support the author (that's me!). If you made it this far, I am offering the digital beta copy of our next book for all customers in hopes for some feedback.

Email me at:
JasonBrownPublishing@gmail.com

Thank you for considering this request. Your words can make a big difference, and together, we can make the Apple world even more accessible and enjoyable for everyone, everywhere!

Thank you,
Jason Brown

COMPANION GUIDE!

If you found our "Macbook Pro and Air for Seniors - A Simple Step-by-Step Guide" helpful, then you'll definitely want to check out our companion guides "iPhone 15 Guide - An Illustrated Step by Step Manual for Seniors".

This guide will help you navigate your iPhone with ease, from sending messages to capturing memories and everything in between.It is specifically designed to make technology accessible for beginners & seniors to confidently dive into the world of technology!

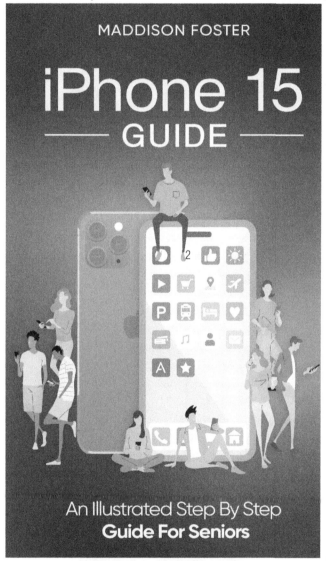

Are you ready to unlock more possibilities? Scan these QR codes on your iPhone and get your copy!

Made in the USA
Las Vegas, NV
22 November 2024